THE P. ...
IN
COMMUNITY AND MINISTRY

THE PARISH IN COMMUNITY AND MINISTRY

Edited and Introduced
by
Evelyn Eaton Whitehead

PAULIST PRESS
New York/Ramsey/Toronto

Library of Congress
Catalog Card Number: 78-58960

ISBN: 0-8091-2133-6

Published by Paulist Press
Editorial Office: 1865 Broadway, New York, N.Y. 10023
Business Office: Island Road, Ramsey , N.J. 07446

Printed and bound in the
United States of America

Contents

If it is true that from the pastoral point of view the parish can no longer be regarded as a closed unit for apostolic work, it would nevertheless be going too fast to conclude from this that the parish is today an obsolete institution. On the contrary, precisely because the canonical parish is open to the supernatural reality of the Church and can be shaped by the changing forms of the world, it is still valid and still has its value as a legal institution. The legal form is in itself adaptable enough to embrace a parish 'congregation' and a parish community and yet to remain responsible for all those who are not yet touched by them. The legal term is by and large flexible enough to be adapted to modern sociological conditions.

Alex Blöchlinger
The Modern Parish Community

Foreword

The laity, religious and clergy who have devoted so much of their lives and talents to the renewal of parish life must be exhilarated that greater interest has been focused more substantially on the parish by bishops, theologians and other scholars in the past few years.

This attention and support is welcome to a degree. There is a caution expressed on the part of parish personnel that they do not want their nascent efforts at renewal and participation smothered by a group of experts or "downtown" types who will descend upon them to tell them how the parish should be "run".

Hard-nosed pastors, experienced sisters and brothers, trained and concerned laity are wary of "experts" and rightfully so after some of their trials and sufferings in the years following Vatican II.

Yet, they know that they need help. They know they need a deeper understanding of the theology of Church, theology of parish, theology of the laity, theology of the priesthood.

They need a great and noble vision of Church as a sign of the Lord working in the world through them and demanding that they give of their lives to the building of a new and finer world which will move all of us into the fullness of life in the Lord.

As parish practitioners need knowledge in theology and skill in theological reflection, they also need skills in human development and systems management which will enable them to build those relationships with others which will, in the present day and in the future, fashion a people who will form communities committed to justice, to love, to growth and freedom, to holiness.

This volume hopes to fill a small gap in our understanding of the parish. We trust that others will continue to explore more of the exciting dimensions of ministry, community and the mission of the local parish.

1

The authors of the chapters in this book are able practitioners in ministry. It is the substance of their work. The common thread which runs through their lives is their caring for people, their ministry to ministers, their constant efforts to produce others who are greater and more zealous than themselves.

This book, hopefully, is the first in a series which will address central questions of ministry in the Church. The volumes which will appear yearly will be written by people of the Church for all those in the Church who believe that the Lord is Our King and Our Shepherd, and who wish to take a part, no matter how small, in the challenging, never ending task of gathering the people, telling the Story, and breaking the Bread.

We hope this series will enable people in parish ministry to perform better—more effectively, more joyfully, more fully. In the future, we plan a volume on the parish as locus of social justice ministries, and another on the relationship of the parish and neighborhood. For, from the parish, with its nourishment in word and sacrament, should go forth people who will dedicate their lives to freeing and healing the individual, the family, the neighborhood, the city and the world.

The inspiration for this volume came primarily from its editors, Drs. James and Evelyn Eaton Whitehead of the University of Notre Dame. Its impetus was the Convocation on Parish Ministry held on the Notre Dame campus in the Fall of 1976.

Through publication of our *Theology in Ministry* series, the Center for Pastoral and Social Ministry at the University of Notre Dame proposes to serve the Church and the University in their common ministry of truth in the service of God and His people.

Msgr. John J. Egan, Director
Center for Pastoral and Social Ministry
University of Notre Dame

Introduction

There are signs of new vitality today in the experience of parish ministry. Through the late '60's and early '70's American Catholics witnessed the enthusiasm of the Vatican II years dissolve into disorder. The parish was not spared this disintegration. The diversity of belief, expectation and expression of faith within single parishes threatened the unity and continuity of this form of Christian life. And local churches were unsure in their responses to both apathy and ardor among their members.

The results of recent scholarship contributed to the malaise. Serious students of the parish pointed to its limitations. In its strict, canonical meaning the parish (*paroecia*) refers first to a territorial division, an artificially designated district.[1] These territorial lines have no necessary relationship to the existing configuration of the local groups of believers. Canonically, the parish is never spoken of as a community. Parishioners (*paroeciani*) are described in terms of the individual relationship of rights and duties each has with the parish priest.

Even our sense that—"traditionally"—the parish is or should be the primary institution of religious expression among the Catholic people is historically naive. As historian Jay Dolan notes, ..."the parish Catholics grew up in during the 1940's and 50's was a relatively recent phenomenon, a product of the 16th century counterreformation that only became normative in Europe toward the end of the 17th century after 150 years of concerted effort on the part of the Catholic hierarchy."[2] Dolan and others[3] argue persuasively that as there are changes in those historical conditions that support the parish as "the sole center of religious life," so there will be a shift away from the image of the local church as a parish-centered institution. The 21st century is likely to see the

3

parish as we know it as only one of several vibrant forms of Christian *ecclesia*.

But, it is the potential of the parish itself as a vibrant form of Christian *ecclesia* that is being newly explored today. A critical moment in the shift from widespread despair concerning parish life to a renewed commitment to its possibility was marked in Bishop Albert Ottenweller's impassioned statement at the 1975 meeting of the National Conference of Catholic Bishops. "I see the parish as the key to renewal in the church," avowed Ottenweller, who has himself ministered as a parish priest for over thirty years. Characterizing himself as "a journeyman pastor," Ottenweller urged that renewed energy be focused on issues of parish life and ministry. "Both the crisis and the challenge lie in the parish," he declared. "My proposal is that parish structure be studied to find a model more adaptable to our time and to the vision of Vatican Council II."

This volume takes up the invitation, the challenge, of Bishop Ottenweller. The book is not directly a discussion of "how to do" parish ministry, nor a review of "what is going on now that is good." Rather it examines several background issues that must be faced as we move toward a clearer understanding of the possibility of the parish in the context of the Christian life in the future. We focus here on three themes, discussing these from several points of view. We treat the parish in its mission, its community, its ministry.

The examination of *The Parish in Community and Ministry* begins in Part One with two essays focusing upon the current experience of parish ministry. These papers highlight issues of ministry and community that are central in the life of the contemporary parish.

In "Parish Ministry: The Old and the New" Bishop Albert Ottenweller challenges the outlook, still current in the practice of many parishes, that sees ministry as the primary or even exclusive concern of the religious professional. "In many ways we have not grown out of that authoritarian, clerical stance in which the pastor stands apart from his people to teach and to give them God's law." The advent of teams of professional ministers may broaden the personnel base, but too often does not alter the paternalistic style of ministry. Ministry remains what the professionals do for the laity.

From St. Paul, and the documents of Vatican II, Ottenweller draws an alternate model of parish ministry. Three convictions stand at its core: ministers rise out of the parish community; there must be ways of discerning what gifts people have for building up the Body of Christ; community ministry is as important as personal ministry. Ottenweller discusses the implications of these convictions for the renewal of parish life. Parishes must be restructured to make spiritual communion possible. Professional ministers must become involved in the development of ministering communities, calling the Christian people to exercise their right to ministry. Both lay persons and professional ministers must develop new skills for the "corporate pilgrimage" which is the ongoing experience of Christian life today.

Sister Paula Ripple continues the analysis of the contemporary experience of parish ministry as she examines "The Promise and the Challenge of Shared Ministry." She looks first at the ministry of Jesus and its embodiment in the communities of the early Church. "Since we must look to these communities that formed around Jesus as the earliest models for parish communities, we need to relate the key aspects of the early communities to the parish communities of our own time." In both the early Church and today the Christian vision demands ministries of healing, teaching and worship. The development of contemporary forms of healing, teaching and worship as shared ministries in the parish setting will require attention to three key concerns. These are questions of planning and ministry, diversity and ministry, and prayerful reflection and ministry. In her discussion of these concerns Ripple returns to her own experience with renewal efforts at the local parish level. Drawing upon this background she demonstrates for us her conclusion: "a parish becomes a ministering community only if its growth and development are creatively planned and prayerfully tended."

In Part Two the analysis of the basic issues of parish ministry and community is continued, now in more explicit dialogue with the resources of contemporary theology and the social sciences.

Community is a conscious goal of many in parish ministry today. In "The Structure of Community" Evelyn Eaton Whitehead examines this goal from a sociological perspective, in an effort to clarify the varied experiences and diverse expectations that complicate the ministry of community formation. Communities are styles of social life that embody some features of "families" and some features of "organizations." But communities are distinctive social forms, involving members in questions of value and providing opportunities for common action as well as mutual support. Whitehead discusses the social form of community in terms of five key characteristics. She closes with a consideration of the role of pluralism, diversity and conflict in community. "Community is begun in the context of communication and commitment to common goals. But it cannot long persist without an active appreciation for diversity within the group and a willingness to face and to resolve the conflicts inevitable in any sustained human relationship."

Theologian John Shea takes up the question of the religious mission of the parish. The question of mission can be addressed only in the context of one's understanding of God, of Christ, and of the Church. The discussion of the mission of the parish must be rooted in a "working ecclesiology," an understanding of the Church which arises in the dialogue of speculative theology with the religious experience and self-awareness of actual communities of believers. "Any understanding of the religious mission of the parish," Shea reminds us, "must be concrete enough to be helpful in creating the structures and programs which are necessary for community living." Shea designates the religious mission of the parish: "to provide the resources and structures for the ongoing interrelating of personal and communal stories with the larger Christian story, for the purposes of redemption." He goes on to sketch the theological understanding of God, Christ, the Church and Christian ministry that supports and gives direction to this mission of the local community of believers.

Gerard Egan deals explicitly with issues of shared ministry raised earlier by Ottenweller and Ripple. In "Ministering Community and Community of Ministers" he scores the "logistic absurdity," implicit in the actual practice of most denominations, that sees officially designated ministers as properly, and even exclusively, responsible for meeting the pastoral needs of the congregation. This "vertical" understanding of ministry must be complemented by an appreciation of "lateral" ministry. "When the members of a parish community, moved by their own initiative and supported and challenged by officially designated ministers, minister to one another, this can be called 'lateral' ministry. When officially designated ministers work to see to it that this kind of initiative is developed among members of the congregation, then they, too, engage in 'lateral' ministry." Drawing upon social and organizational psychology, Egan discusses the principles of leadership and organization that can assist the parish in its move toward an effective life as a ministering community.

In "The Parish as Locus of Liturgical Ministries" Daniel Coughlin examines the interrelations that exist in the parish between liturgy and ministry. "In every parish the Sunday Eucharist is the celebration of multiple ministries," Coughlin begins. He goes on to show the power of the parish's liturgical experience to invite, acknowledge, form, affirm and celebrate—at both the practical and symbolic levels—the needs and gifts of the community. "As locus of liturgical ministries," Coughlin concludes, "every parish has the potential for enabling its people to grow spiritually, to assume responsibilities and begin to serve others, to grasp the concept and the experience of ministry." Thus the liturgy serves as an efficacious sacrament of community, both expressing and nourishing the life and ministry of the parish.

Philip Murnion continues the analysis of the parish as community in "Parish as Source of Community and Identity." For both the individual and the group, religious identity is rooted in the experience of church community. The local church, the parish, is essentially a symbolic value community. Parish ministry must be concerned with those symbols and values that illumine religious meaning, deepen religious commitment, and motivate religious action among believing women and men of this time and place. Murnion recalls the parish of the past, noting those factors that contributed to its serving as a comprehensive value community for its members. He goes on to examine current needs and developments within Catholic Church life that suggest the future shape of the parish as a religious value community.

Each of the contributors to this volume has served in ministry in the parish setting. Most remain currently involved in parish ministry, on a full-time or part-time basis. It is upon this fund of experience as well as upon analysis and reflection that their considerations here are based.

This book is part of a larger effort within the Church today, the struggle to discover structures of Christian life together that are more adequate to our present and more worthy of our future. It is dedicated to the women and men who participate in that struggle.

Evelyn Eaton Whitehead

NOTES

1. *Codex Iuris Canonici,* can. 216, par. 1. For a discussion of parish as the term is found in canon law, see Alex Blöchlinger, *The Modern Parish Community* (New York: P.J. Kenedy and Sons, 1964), pp. 32-33, 109-119.

2. "The Parish-Past and Present," Special Insert, *National Catholic Reporter,* May 31, 1974. For fuller discussion of the history of the American Catholic parish, see also Dolan's *The Immigrant Church: New York's Irish and German Catholics, 1815-1865* (Baltimore: Johns Hopkins University Press, 1975) and *Catholic Revivalism: The American Experience, 1830-1900* (Notre Dame, In.: Notre Dame Press, 1977).

3. Bernard Cooke, *The Ministry of Word and Sacrament* (Philadelphia: Fortress Press, 1976), p. 21; James H. Provost, "Structuring the Community," *Chicago Studies*, 15 (Fall, 1976), pp. 271-273; David O'Brien, *The Renewal of American Catholicism* (New York: Oxford Press, 1972).

Part I
The Experience of
Parish Ministry:
Defining the Issues

Parish Ministry:
The Old and the New

Albert Ottenweller

Recently I was invited to the University of Notre Dame as an observer at a convocation on parish ministry. My qualifications to participate included my 34 years experience in pastoral ministry as well as my being a bishop who still serves as pastor in a parish.

The meeting brought together crack parish ministry teams from all over the U.S. They represented a diversity of ministries and pastoral settings. Teams came from suburban parishes, rural parishes, inner-city parishes, and ethnic parishes. They were distinguished for providing what was judged to be the finest, most creative ministry available to the American Church in our time.

As I moved among the groups, listening to discussions and hearing programs described, I was impressed with the variety of ministries these teams represented and the creative things they were about. I felt, though, there was a basic flaw in the way their ministries were performed. Though the teams were professional and efficient, they were still following what I believe is a pre-Vatican II outlook on ministry. I know that outlook well. I practiced that kind of ministry for most of my priesthood.

In the parish the pastor was responsible for ministry. It was as if he had a line running from himself to each parishioner. He felt responsible for visiting each one, caring for all the sick, dispensing the sacraments, making the moral decisions, giving pastoral advice, etc. In the minds of most people the priest was the Church. And generally, this "Father-does-and-knows-best" condition was acceptable to the parishioners. If the pastor was responsible for

11

ministry, then they did not have to be. The parish was primarily his concern.

At the convocation, as I listened to the pastoral teams, I got the impression that they were continuing this paternalistic type of ministry; only now, substituting "team" for "pastor." The team has a line to every parishioner. The team visits the poor, cares for the sick, gives pastoral advice; perhaps more thoroughly, more efficiently, but in the same traditional style.

As I read the documents of Vatican II, I see a vision of ministry different from this. I rejoice to hear that the Church is called the People of God. In "Lumen Gentium" I hear echoes of St. Paul's words to the Corinthians: "There are different gifts, but the same Spirit; there are different ministries, but the same Lord; there are different works, but the same God . . . . You, then, are the Body of Christ. Everyone of you is a member of it. Furthermore, God has set up in the Church, first apostles, second prophets, third teachers, then miracle workers, healers, assistants, administrators, and those who speak in tongues. Are all apostles? Are all prophets? Are all teachers?" (1 Cr. 12)

Paul does not see the pastor (team) as having all the gifts. Each member has gifts given for the good of the Body. Each uses his gifts for the building up of the Body. It is not the priest (team) that is important. It is the Body of Christ, the parish.

If I think of ministry in terms of Paul's model, certain important ideas surface in my mind: 1) Ministers rise out of the parish community; 2) There must be a way of discerning what gifts people have for building up the Body of Christ; 3) Community ministry might be as important as personal ministry.

For several years I have been working in my own parish in an effort to remodel its structure. I believe that the traditional parish structure is too institutional, too authoritarian, too impersonal. I believe strongly that people today are hungry. They are hungry for friendship, hungry for celebration, hungry for God. People today are searching. They are searching for a group with whom they can live together in faith, searching for something that calls them to worship, searching for ways they can enter more deeply into themselves. And people today are filled with longing. They are longing for a place they can call home, longing for people who are truly their brothers and sisters in Christ, longing for a spiritual family in which they can risk being themselves and where they will be willing to give their lives for one another.

The years of remodelling have been a struggle. Those of us who joined forces in this effort have had many failures, have made many mistakes. By our experience, though, we have learned important lessons. One of my greatest thrills in the struggle was to experience what happened when small groups of Catholics were able to be in faith relationships over a considerable period of time. Alfred was a meat cutter in a super market. He was shy, uncommunicative. The only indication of spiritual motivation was that he and his wife, Barbara, took in foster children from the local juvenile court. They happened to join a formation group in our parish which we called the pre-catechumenate. For nine months they were in a sharing group of ten adults within the larger context of 25 families committed to one another. As the months went on, we could see Alfred grow. It was like a new life dawning. He felt at home with the others in his group. As his trust grew he was able to express the feelings that were in him; how he experienced life, how he felt about prayer, his frustrations about parish life.

He gradually felt more confident about himself. He grew excited about the possibilities of the Gospel message for his family and his neighbors. There were beliefs and ideas he felt so strongly about that he was willing to stand up for them. Al and Barbara felt called to carry the message of the Gospel to their neighborhood. They invited neighbors to their home, talked with them about parish problems, shared with them the exciting possibilities of communion in the neighborhood. Neighbors read the scriptures together, celebrated anniversaries together, took down their backyard fences to make a common playground for their children. All the time Al was still his shy self, staying in the background.

Others, however, recognized his gift of leadership. He was nominated and elected to the parish council. After two years he was elected president of the parish council. It was highly unusual in this parish for a meat cutter to hold a post of this kind, but the most exciting thing was Al's grasp of what parish should mean. He had an uncanny instinct about what the ordinary parishioner felt and a beautiful vision of what he might become.

One warm night after a parish meeting, Al and the priests were sitting around the kitchen table enjoying a beer and Al said, "You guys have got to be careful when you put the hand on someone's shoulder. There's a fellow in our neighborhood who'd give you the shirt off his back. He's a super guy, but he doesn't go to church, or give any money to the church. You know why? You guys put the hand on his boss's shoulder. You made him a big church fella, because he gave you discounts on cars and bowed and scraped when you came into his garage. At the same time, though, he was underpaying his help and treating them bad.

"I argued with myself a long time before I took the job as council president, because now I'm a church person. I'm a marked man with many rank and file members of the parish."

Al came up from the ranks. Nobody, least of all himself, knew that he had gifts of leadership and insight. He was inarticulate. He felt deeply about things, but was unable to express himself. It was in communion with his brothers and sisters that he discovered himself and others discovered him. I thought I could teach him about ministry, but as it turned out, he taught me. Today he stands with his neighbors as before, but there is a difference. He is one with them, not only able to, but wanting to call them to communion, to that mutual sharing of one another's presence which is Christ.

The full stature of Alfred's growth in his understanding of his role in the parish can best be described in the following incident. As a parish leader who guides and supports the Parish Renewal formation teams (they work on programs for the remodeling of the parish), Alfred summed up his feelings at a recent team meeting. "You know all of this time we have given the power and responsibility for deciding the future of our parish to transients. The priest and sisters have come in, made all of the decisions and then they have moved on. And we are the ones who must live with them. Don't misunderstand me. The decisions were made in good faith. We've had good leaders, but I know now that I have a responsibility and I can bring something that none of them can. I need to be part of the decision making, too."

If we are really serious about developing lay ministers, we must move beyond simply communicating new information—new images of ministry, new models of the Church. In a real sense ministry, as religion itself, cannot be taught. It must be experienced. True, for ministry, people must learn certain skills, must have knowledge of scripture and theology; but God save us from the "professionals." The skills and knowledge can become tools that create greater alienation. Unless skills and knowledge are learned in relationship to the real situation of the parish, more pockets of isolation will be created. When we take people out of the community of the parish into the artificial environment of the classroom, the candidates for ministry tend to become "clericalized." They see their information, their learning experiences as separate from themselves and the community in which they live, or they see them as a means to "save" the rest of the community. As many deacons have, they tend to detach themselves from the ranks of the laity and join the priests and sisters as "over against." How different from Alfred's invitation to share life and learn together with those he serves. It is in the very milieu of parish with its love and joy, pain and struggle, that the man or woman becomes aware of what it means to minister. As he grows in this awareness he, himself, will be the one to ask for training in skills and theology.

It is my sense that the parish structure is so outmoded that it becomes a painful work place for priest, sisters and lay people, or a waiting ground for better forms of ministry. This unhappy condition tempts many to bypass the parish. I remember the temptation to bypass began with me long ago in the heyday of the Christian Family Movement. We used to meet in homes with the grudging permission of the pastor. We grew fond of each other. We shared much in discussing liturgy, scripture and the apostolate. When we agreed on an action, however, often we ran headlong into clerical opposition and the action died. It was so frustrating for all of us to see clearly what action should be taken, to be willing to commit ourselves to that action, and then to be prevented from seeing it realized. Wouldn't it be easier to go another way?

Cursillo, Marriage Encounter and Charismatic Movement are very alive and thrilling in their possibilities for growth in love and the Spirit. In no way would I want to be critical of what these movements have accomplished. Each in its own fashion has made significant contributions to the renewal of the Catholic Church in the U.S. I believe, however, that they have prospered precisely because they offered people a communion they could not find in their own parish. Parishioners had to leave their parish to have their hearts touched by an experience of community.

As a transitional stage in renewal these movements are important, but in the long run the Church will suffer unless we face the unhappy condition of the parish and enter the struggle to reconstruct it so that the parish itself will be home and family to the faithful.

It is sad to me that so much talent among Christians is hidden and unused. Gifts are unknown even by persons who possess them. Parishes, as presently structured, have difficulty discovering talent in people. Even when this talent is discovered, there is often difficulty putting it meaningfully to use. I know a young couple who are well educated and have a wealth of experience in working with the poor. The husband had been in the Peace Corps for several years. The wife had been Head Start coordinator in a fairly large city. The two of them were so highly motivated that after their marriage they quit their jobs and moved to Washington, D.C. which they thought of as the nerve center of our country, with the intention to devote their lives to the service of their brothers and sisters. When they arrived in the city they volunteered their services in several parishes. Nowhere, they told me, could they find a parish where they were needed in a meaningful ministry. I have heard deacons say that after they have gone through an intensive training program, and have been ordained for parish service, they are frustrated because their pastors cannot find anything meaningful for them to do.

It is as though we cannot move beyond the stereotype of lay minister as catechism teacher, or distributor of communion, or assistant at the altar. It is as though we are blind to the signs of the times that surround us. Today a host of people leave the Church because it has failed to recognize their presence in the parish. It is naive to think that the priest or even the team will be able to make all the contacts, to initiate and to maintain all the relationships that make up the life-vital parish. But our operating mentality seems to still be that this is the proper task of the priest or the team alone.

I know of a woman living one block from the Church whose husband is an alcoholic and often violent. She visited the pastor once but is afraid and ashamed to go again. Whose responsibility is it to care and support her and the millions like her?

We encourage people to attend Cursillo, Marriage Encounter and Parish Retreats. They come home deeply touched, eager to share their experiences and ready for commitment, and often we offer them only the "ministry" of bingo. How long is it before their disappointment leads them to abandon us? More and more our most creative leaders are using their energies elsewhere than the parish.

There is a movement in our land for ordination of women. I do not pretend to understand all the dimensions of the movement, but I hear in it a cry of deep frustration. I hear a plea from a woman to be able to share her gifts, her yearning to author life, her sensitivity to heal, her special call of the Spirit that she recognizes deep within her own personhood. A parish of shared community would call forth the gifts of womanhood, so much more happily than does the present institutional one.

It seems to me that we need to set aside our basic assumptions concerning ministry and begin to dream; hard dreams, creative dreams, challenging dreams that will provide the heart of a new theology of ministry rooted in an old theology—the New Testament. We need to consider ways of helping one another discover our gifts. More, we need to determine a rhythm of life within the parish in which the discovery of our giftedness is as much a part of its pattern as is Baptism or Sunday liturgy. We need to dream until we rediscover that ministry is not some specific thing we do, but a way we live together. It is the call of the Spirit within each of us to live the Gospel life, to live in communion with our brothers and sisters, to be warmly human and sensitive people with eyes that see and ears that hear and hearts that are willing to understand. We need to dream about ministry until we begin to see that it is everyone's right and that we, the full-time, professional ministers, must be about calling people to exercise that right.

If we hope to improve the involvement of people in the ministry of the parish we must renew the parish in such a way that it will be less heavily institutional and more given to communion. It is not that the institutional components of the parish should be cast aside. The resources that the institution provides are necessary in order that we may stay in touch with our traditions and provide programs and personnel for service. It is to communion, however, that the parish is being called. Jesus gave us the two commandments: Love God with your whole heart; Love your neighbor as yourself. The purpose of the institutional Church on every level—the Vatican, the diocese, and the parish—is to facilitate the communion of the faithful, people together with God and with one another.

Communion is so vital in our times because of our loneliness. Mother Teresa has said that in India people are plagued with hunger even unto death because of the lack of food. But, in the United States, the richest country in the world, there is a more gnawing hunger, the hunger of loneliness. In the Church we have an ideal theology of community and a poor practice of community.

It is no longer possible for us to fulfill our obligation to charity just by giving money or by working in the ghetto. The time has come when we must give nothing less than our own selves, our weaknesses, our strengths, all that we are.

In his encyclical "Ecclesiam Suam" Paul VI symbolizes the Church as the Dialogue of Salvation. He says, "The world cannot be saved from the outside. As the Word of God became man, so must a man to a certain degree identify himself with the forms of life of those to whom he wishes to bring the message of Christ. Without invoking privileges which would but widen the separation, without employing unintelligible terminology, he must share the common way of life—provided that it is human and honorable—especially of the most humble, if he wishes to be listened to and understood.

"And before speaking, it is necessary to listen, not only to a man's voice, but to his heart. A man must first be understood; and, where he merits it, agreed with. In the very act of trying to make ourselves pastors, fathers and teachers of men, we must make ourselves their brothers. The spirit of dialogue is friendship and, even more, is service. All this we must remember and strive to put into practice according to the example and commandment that Christ left to us."

It seems to me that we are still trying in our parishes to put the

new wine in the old bottles. We are still pre-Vatican II in our
pastoral instincts. In many ways we have not grown out of that
authoritarian, clerical stance in which the pastor, as it were, stood
apart from his people to teach and give them God's law. When I
was a young assistant I always marvelled at the power of the
pastor. On Sunday morning he would stand in the pulpit (the
church held 1,400 people) and give the faithful the orders for the
week. He expected and received, as far as we knew, full com-
pliance. There was never any real consultation. People would see a
crew of workmen using a power shovel to dig a huge hole in the
ground. They would ask, "What's going on?" "We're building an
addition to the High School." That was his form of communication.

In effect, the parish was the pastor's and the parishioners
belonged to it and to him. As Archbishop Paul Hallinan has noted,
the symbol of the Church as a triangle with the Pope at the top, the
Bishops in the middle and the people at the bottom was pleasing to
the eye, but did nothing for the heart. Better, he suggests, is a new
symbol, the circle where all work and pray together in communion.

Many important things are being said today about community.
Yet it seems to me that very little is being done to redesign the
parish according to the vision of the Council. It is as if we are in a
state of shock. Are we afraid that the parish is so brittle with age
that it will disintegrate if we disturb it? Are priests and religious
threatened at the serious prospect of calling lay people to ministry?
Are we waiting for Vatican II to go away? Vatican II will not go
away, but the people of our parishes may well.

In his book *Be Not Afraid* Jean Vanier speaks to the situation
of many people today: "It is when people are not taught to pray and
to enter into the mystical movement of Christianity, when they are
not called forth to experience real love, that they turn to other
pastures which do not really nourish. They turn away because they
have not learned from their shepherd how to communicate with
God, how to listen to the Spirit, how to discern the things which are
of God and the things which are not. They have not received that
which is essential to nourish their thirst for the Eternal and for the
liberty which comes from Jesus. They do not know this truth which
will set them free, the Spirit of God who liberates from fear and
from law. They do not know how the Spirit will teach freedom so

that they may grow in love and commitment, loving truth, refusing all the compromise that brings shadows and darkness upon the light. If people do not sense this force of light in the shepherd, they will turn to other pastures, whether these are drugs, a world of violence and revolution or of other political theories, or the seeking of relationships only through sexuality. If there is no real pasture, people will die of depression, of starvation. They will die thirsting."

If we agree that the quality of ministry in the parish will be in proportion to the depth of communion, then the first order of business must be renewing the structures of the parish to make spiritual communion possible. We must take up the struggle within the parish itself. This is such a priority to me that I believe we ought to lay aside all but essential programs to give time and personnel to this effort.

We cannot wait until such renewal is mandated from above. The effort is best initiated from the bottom up rather than from the top down. Updating the parish will not be effected simply by reading books, nor by attending workshops and conferences. It will be accomplished by groups of lay people, religious and clergy working in consort with one another. This renewal is not a one-time effort nor a packaged program, but an ongoing process at the very heart of the Christian experience, a process by which we must continually seek to rediscover our communion around a common mission.

Many individual Christians today are making a personal pilgrimage to God. I think laity, religious and clergy of a parish must make a spiritual pilgrimage together, gradually becoming aware of who they are as a people called and redeemed by Christ. This corporate pilgrimage calls for new skills in interpersonal relationships. The Body of Christ is not just people getting together, but people living corporately in terms of communion and the Gospel message.

I have a friend who says, "If you are going to turn an elephant over, you'd better have a damned good grip on the elephant." The time has come for us to tackle the elephant. We have been busy about many good programs and movements, but reconstructing the parish is the one challenge that is crucial to the future.

The Promise and the Challenge of Shared Ministry

Paula Ripple

"We live our lives forward, but we understand them backwards." These words of Kierkegaard reflect fairly accurately the dynamic of my own understanding of the parish. It has been over ten years since the Second Vatican Council, a decade filled with experimentation and activity in parish experience. For the past five years I have been a member of a parish ministerial team. I have participated with, and attempted to serve, a group of fellow Christians in our common struggle to become a ministering community, sharing and caring for one another in ways reflective of the invitation of Jesus. Now I am invited to "understand backwards," to think about what has happened to me and to those with whom I have shared both my vision of lived Christianity and my life. It is out of these experiences and reflections that my conclusions about the parish have deepened and become clearer.

At the time of Vatican II, the Church and the nature of the Church were redefined. There emerged a much-expanded definition of the place of lay people and non-ordained ministers in the life of the Church. Today, few would argue with the important place lay people have, or at least ought to have, in the Church. Unfortunately, using words about ministry and leadership while failing to identify, clarify, develop and support this leadership has created unfair expectations and unfulfilled hopes in the development of parish communities. People with important gifts to bring have heard words spoken about their expanded role, while they have experienced key decisions being made without them. From the vantage point of both the people and those in pastoral roles, this

21

Vatican II vocabulary is often confusing and devoid of meaning.

Nearly ten years after Vatican II we are discovering that some vital steps were missed in the enthusiasm immediately following the Council. We spoke of shared leadership but we failed, in the practical setting of the parish, to work out systematically what the appropriate parameters and goals of this leadership were to be. We failed to provide for the kinds of studied support and guidance needed to help parish members shift, from being people who had no voice in the parish to being people who assume responsibility for the major decisions that give vision and direction to a parish community. We failed to clarify some basic scriptural and theological understandings of the Church. Without this clarification parishes can become centers of activity that lack the direction which grows from a clear sense of mission and well-defined goals. These goals must be established in an environment of prayerful reflection on the meaning of the Gospel, and particularly of our fundamental commitment in baptism to be a faith-centered community. We come together in Jesus' name to test our personal values against the values he exemplified in his own life. We search for community in the light of the values he set forth for those communities which grew up around him.

If we ask the question, "how does a parish become a ministering community?", my experience tells me that we might answer simply by saying, "only with great difficulty." But this response is not very satisfactory. Let us look at it another way. To derive some sense of direction from Vatican Council II regarding the parish and how it comes to be a ministering community, it is important for a parish staff to work with the people to develop a sense of leadership that is helpful to them and productive for the parish. In any parish there are many practical and administrative tasks that must be done. Even these tasks serve community better when they are informed with a sense of vision that makes it possible for people to see themselves as more than mere functionaries. We must help people to understand what they are doing in a new way. We must help them develop a vision that sees even the most ordinary tasks of parish life as a part of the variety of gifts of the community of which St. Paul speaks. This means establishing a wider perspective of pastoral ministry. This means expanding the understanding of who the parish's ministers are.

The Model of Jesus' Ministry

If we recall the early Church and look at Jesus and Paul as they were forming new communities, we find these communities were not just groups of people who gathered around Jesus or Paul to do certain tasks. Nor did Jesus accumulate crowds around himself so that he could minister to them. He did not communicate to them that he was the minister and they were being ministered to. We find Jesus consistently reminding those who followed him that "I have not called you my servants but my friends." (Jn 15:15) He invited them to share in his own ministry. He urged them to be ready to do as he was doing. He said, "As the Father has sent me, so I am sending you . . . . " (Jn 17:18) Jesus gave to his followers a sense of their own ministry so that those who spent time with him were able to leave him to go and form new communities. The rapid and enthusiastic growth of the early small communities speaks to just how well Jesus was able to give people the gift of ministry. It reminds us of how he communicated to them the message of their worth in such a way that they understood their personal responsibility to be present to others and to minister to one another. Dynamic and loved as Jesus was, he gave to others the ability to give themselves.

If we look carefully at these early communities and at the ministry of Jesus, we find that there were three aspects to the community life that he encouraged and developed; namely, healing, teaching and worship. The stories of Jesus' healing are numerous in sacred scripture. They remind us that those who wrote the stories of Jesus after his death spoke of those qualities about Jesus that they most remembered. It is clear that people came to Jesus and stayed with him because they sought healing not only for their bodies but also for their spirits. The gospels tell us that the apostles and those who worked with Jesus also healed and were looked to for healing. And, we have Jesus' constant reminder to his early followers, "As I have done and been for you, so I invite you to do and be for one another." (Jn 12:15)

We find Jesus teaching by telling stories that help people understand their own lives, their relationship with the Father and with each other. He encouraged his followers not only to listen carefully to what he was telling them, but also to share that teaching with others. "Go, and make followers of all nations, teaching them to understand all that I have taught you. Do this in the name of the Father and of the Son and of the Holy Spirit." (Mt 28:19)

In addition to healing and teaching, we find Jesus praying alone and sharing prayer with others. We find him setting all that he does in the context of his relationship with his Father. We find prayer and worship to be central to Jesus' life and built into the life that he shared with those who came to follow and to stay with him.

Since we must look to these communities that formed around Jesus as the earliest models for parish communities, we need to relate the key aspects of the early communities to the parish communities of our own time.

The healing dimension of Jesus' ministry speaks to us of our need to be concerned about an experience of healing that goes beyond physical well-being. This healing transcends the boundaries of parish community and extends to the widest dimensions of world community. It challenges us to look at our parish communities to determine in what ways and to what extent the special needs of all persons are being tended. Missionaries in foreign lands have come to realize that one cannot effectively preach God's word to starving and hurting bodies with basic survival needs. We are only gradually learning in parish communities that the response to parish education programs and other parish activities that may be expected is impossible when families are existing in emotional and psychological survival patterns. Education programs are not the primary concern of families suffering from one or many of the destructive cultural pressures affecting homes and marriages today. An important aspect of parish community is the tending, in a variety of ways, of the human needs within the parish.

Since community is a challenge much wider than one's own parish, some continual consciousness-raising and vision-widening in response to Jesus' invitation to heal is the responsibility of the decision-makers in every parish. To allow a narrow, and somewhat comfortable, vision of community, as caring only for the needs of the people within that single parish is to betray the vision of Jesus who reminds us that every person's cares are our responsibility and the proper object of our shared life.

Jesus' injunction to teach has been understood and responded to in most parish communities. But the fact that widespread teaching occurs, either through a Catholic school or in parish CCD programs, is not necessarily an indication that we have understood this message fully. While many see the formal teaching of religion as the responsibility of the parish and the wider church, fewer people understand that any area of human life is the proper object of parish education programs. We have often insisted that "the supernatural works through the natural" and yet, in subtle ways, we continue to look upon certain kinds of topics as "appropriate" for parish education and others as "not appropriate." Again, if we take Jesus as our model, if we look at the parables he used and the teaching for which he is remembered, we discover that education was, for him, far wider and deeper than simply using some words about his Father and about how we would be worthy to live with his Father. Following the example of Jesus, we need to do the broadest possible instruction about church, community, values, human communication, family and marriage, parenting skills, work and business ethics, emotions and emotional life, human sexuality, world hunger, care of the earth, and understanding justice as a gospel value. In the light of this, it is clear that adult education, and not that of small children, is the central focus and most important parish education commitment.

Finally, we need to think carefully and plan wisely for the possibility of rich and effective worship in our parish communities in following the model of the early communities that formed around Jesus. We have understood, even though in too narrow a way, the parish responsibility to provide for education. We have sometimes understood neither the healing dimension of Jesus' mission nor a community sense of worship as being equally vital. A variety of workshops to provide information and a wide experience of various forms of worship are basic to the growth of a sense of community within a parish. Without this sense of prayer and worship, without the shared experience of searching for and finding God, there is the risk of losing the way and of forgetting what is at the heart of religious experience. Without this sense of prayer even the best planned liturgies remain meaningless.

The Contemporary Parish as a Ministering Community

Given the present structures and the time in which we live in the Church, I believe that a parish becomes a ministering community

——IF there is clear invitation, encouragement and support from the pastor.

——IF the diversity of needs and gifts of the community are dealt with openly and honestly.

——IF listening is a high priority for all.

——IF there is a competent and dedicated professional staff.

——IF there is an atmosphere of trust.

——IF there is long-range planning.

——IF clear goals are set for the entire parish.

——IF committees and other work groups support the goals and establish measurable objectives helpful in reaching the goals.

——IF groups who are active in the parish take time to tend their group as well as to do the task at hand.

——IF there is an ongoing process for defining roles and areas of responsibility.

——IF all of this is done in an atmosphere that is prayerful and conscious of God's presence as a loving environment.

——IF there is openness to the presence of the Spirit of Jesus, as a challenging growing edge.

——IF it is done in companionship with Jesus who also struggled with the joyful and painful ways in which ministry and community are the responsibility of all.

These elements can be summarized under three key concerns: (1) planning and ministry, (2) diversity and ministry, and, (3) prayerful reflection and ministry. We might speak of the first as establishing goals, of the second as clarifying roles, and of the third as processing the experience. In the course of all that has preceded this, I have actually spoken of these three areas. I want to re-emphasize them now in this context and spell out more clearly what I see as vital to each.

Planning and Ministry: Establishing Goals

Both long and short range planning are crucial if a parish is to be a place where people can, and do, minister to one another with compassion, with consistency, and with an awareness that they do so always in Jesus' name. Unless responsibility is taken for insuring that long-range planning occurs I believe that a parish will find itself (or lose itself) far from any meaningful contact with the message of the gospel. This long-range planning begins with a thorough needs assessment. Any planning done without determining parish needs may mean that the people most in need of ministry (and that includes all of us at one time or another) will never receive it. Unless the results of this needs assessment are shared with the entire parish, the finance committee that must translate these needs into projected dollar costs will have a difficult time communicating and selling its plans to the people in the pews. Unless there is adequate communication of needs, the work of any committee related to the basic areas of healing, teaching or worship stands the chance of having its work cut back, temporarily halted, or totally cut off by budgetary decisions made out of necessity when the parish council decides what it can and cannot afford to do on the basis of how much money is available at budget time.

Experience indicates that people respond well to the process of planning for parish needs. People respond to needs that are presented in the context of the growth of their own parish community. If budgetary decisions are made for several consecutive years without projected planning, it may well be discovered much too late that things have been cut off that the parish needs if it is serious about being a ministering community. Unless a parish community reflects on why it chooses certain goals and priorities along the way, the precious vision of the early communities of Jesus slips away in a nearly imperceptible manner. The direction in which the parish moves becomes unsure.

Diversity and Ministry: Clarifying Goals

St. Paul spoke often of the "many gifts but one Spirit of Jesus" (I Cor. 12:4) as important to the life of his communities. This ideal of diversified gifts is beautiful, as is the power that is manifest in a community where there are creative talents used in concert. But parish experience tells us that there is a nearly direct ratio between the quality of the enthusiasm and creativity and the possibility for conflict and tension. This is not a pessimistic statement. It is an honest observation, an observation growing out of the learned insight that tension and conflict need not be destructive. In fact, the potential quality of parish ministry is related directly to the strength and diversity of the gifts of its members. This is precisely why it is important for roles to be clarified if there is a serious desire to carry out an extensive and effective ministry.

There are many ways of looking at the variety of gifts and roles within a parish community. The most obvious roles that need to be considered are the following: the pastor, the professional staff, the parish council, and the committees.

I have mentioned earlier and wish to restate my belief that, given the present structures and the time in which we live, the key person determining the direction of the parish is the pastor. There are those who wish that this were different. There are others who say that the pastor is not important. The truth is that neither of the above attitudes is realistic. For the people or the staff to function as though the pastor is not in a key role is calculated to result in either disillusionment or conflict. For some people this may result in their leaving the mainstream of parish activity.

The post-Vatican II shift was away from the pastor as the chief magistrate and the source of all knowledge. The nature of the parish structure and the manner in which a parish operates remains one in which the pastor's role is central. From the point of view of the larger church, the pastor is in the key leadership position. This leadership need not be dictatorial. Hopefully it can call forth life while taking appropriate responsibility.

When I hear pastors say that there is no place for them in the parish now, or when I hear them ask someone else to define their role, I am concerned about the abdication of responsibilities that are appropriately theirs. When this pastoral abdication happens, a parish risks moving into confusion. In this confusion it is not likely that the people will develop a sense of their own ministry.

As a staff member, and as a woman in a pastoral role, I recognize the appropriate place for the pastor's leadership. Certainly the style of leadership that is needed from pastors is very different and more exacting than it was when all the decision-making was centered in the pastor. To assume responsibility for coordinating and calling forth the gifts of a ministering community requires adjustment to a new style of ministry. Sharing the pastoral role not only with the rest of the staff but with members of the parish, testing the vision of parish community and church, establishing a climate for a ministering community—these are at the heart of the pastor's role. He must clearly understand his role before he can help other people to understand theirs.

Every person active in the parish needs a well-defined concept of his or her responsibilities and of the expectations of others. The staff, the members of the parish council and committee members need to engage in serious dialog to work out, in a mutually acceptable way, what the tasks of each will be and where accountability rests.

Since the Second Vatican Council, I have observed that the model for parish community that is too generally accepted, though perhaps subconsciously, is that of the racetrack. People are seen and are spoken of as being "ahead of" or "behind" others. We use the terms progressive and conservative as though progress in Christian community were marked in much the same manner that it is marked on a racetrack. Racetracks are places of competition. They are not places where relationship is a value. To the extent that any one person, or group, see themselves as ahead of or behind others in the parish, the possibility of community is restricted. I believe that the challenge of parish communities is to replace the symbol of the racetrack with the symbol of the circle as appropriate for a ministering community. In a circle, none are ahead of or behind, all stand in relation to one another. The circle is a symbol of completeness, not competition. It includes all. It is a place where each has value.

For any parish community to replace the symbol of the racetrack with the symbol of the circle it is necessary to recognize the diversity that exists, to clarify the roles of persons bringing their gifts, and to cherish the gifts of others in such a way that ministry is shared, is given and is received.

Prayerful Reflection and Ministry:
Processing the Experience

To ask the question, "How does a parish become a ministering community?" is to ask a question that must, necessarily, find its answer in God's word. The gospels take us back to our deepest roots in Christian community. They put us in contact with the earliest Christian communities when the Followers of the Way learned from Jesus the meaning of his words, "Where two or three are gathered in my name . . . . " (Mt. 18:20) There is a difference between groups of people coming together in the name of many activities and those of us who gather because we choose to live our lives as Jesus did. Hans Kung refers to Christianity as a call to live a "radical humanism" after the manner of Jesus.

As Christians we will not find meaning for our lives unless our human experience is continually processed in self-reflection and in a context of prayerful attention to the meaning of Jesus' life. At the heart of meaningful ministry is the need for quiet time and space in which to test our lives and their direction against the truest touchstone we have, which is the life of Jesus.

To the extent that a parish community understands itself as a pilgrim people always on the way, always undergoing some change and some need for re-evaluation, to that extent the parish insures its own investment in becoming a community which truly ministers. This means that the process we have discussed can never be looked upon as "finished." It demands an ongoing commitment from all who carry the concerns in a parish community.

Conclusion

It is my conviction that the parish is presently the place in which the richest forms of shared ministry can be experienced. In the efforts in parish ministry that I have known over the past decade, in all its successes and failures, I have witnessed hundreds of people who have come to a deeper sense of themselves as ministers in a ministering community. I have experienced a high quality of leadership training and I have seen the development of individual gifts.

The people and not the professional staff are the ongoing reality of the parish. Recognizing their own and each other's gifts, our people are growing in their understanding of the parish not as a place where people are ministered to by a pastor or a professional staff, but as a place where every member of the community has gifts that are important to the lives of the other members.

Parishes do not become ministering communities because some of the right words have been spoken and written by the council fathers and others. People do not come to an understanding of their own role in parish ministry simply because they are committed and willing to be involved. A parish becomes a ministering community only if its growth and development are creatively planned and prayerfully tended.

Part II
The Analysis of
Parish Ministry:
Exploring the Themes

The Structure of Community: Toward Forming the Parish As a Community of Faith

Evelyn Eaton Whitehead

The Catholic parish today is being called to community. Some of the voices sound from within the Church. One of the most significant declarations of Vatican II has been its call for the Church to understand itself as the people of God and to experience its life as a life together in community. This vision of Christian life challenges the sometimes impersonal and often outmoded structures that many experience as the parish. Unofficial prayer groups and informal liturgies serve the religious needs of those for whom the more official activities of the parish seem empty and irrelevant.

But voices outside the Church are heard as well. Observers of the American scene note an increasing privatism in family life and fracturing of social ties. These factors contribute to the experience on the part of many Americans of distance and impotence in the face of the larger social world. Through the periods of immigration over the past century, the Catholic parish has served many as a context of belonging and social involvement that diminished this sense of alienation. If it is able to revitalize its function as a social community, these analysts argue, the parish may go on to make a unique contribution to the American democracy—one that is crucial to the societal as well as to the religious life of the nation.[1]

These ideals of the parish as a community can generate a renewed commitment on the part of those in Christian ministry whose locus is the parish. But these ideals can also serve as stumbling blocks. The goal of community can seem too distant from the facts of parish life that one experiences; the task of community formation, too monumental; the gap between the rhetoric and the reality, too broad to be bridged.

Recent efforts to move parishes toward more communal forms of interaction have been neither easy nor very successful. Many reasons are offered to explain this difficulty—numbers, apathy, distance, time, inertia. The explanation perhaps runs deeper. Perceptive critics of American life have underscored a contemporary ambivalence regarding community.[2] An expressed desire to live in trust and fraternal cooperation stands alongside an enduring cultural commitment to individualism and the autonomous pursuit of one's own destiny. American Catholics have not been spared the experience of these cultural contradictions. For American Catholics the term "community" is vague, even confusing. For some, community seems to call for a return to a kind of neighborliness and interdependence that is thought (perhaps only nostalgically) to have characterized small town America or the ethnically-defined urban neighborhood. For others, community suggests the family or a similar intimate network of people. Here Christian community would seem to include the development of close ties in an atmosphere of personal sharing and mutual support.

When the Church speaks of itself—in its formal documents, in its liturgical texts and homilies—it often does so in the language of intimate family life. We are called upon to love one another, to care for each other's needs, to act toward each other as friends, to view ourselves as members of the same family. But for many contemporary observers of the Church this language seems to stand in direct contradiction to their experience of the Church as an institution. From this perspective the Church is not a family. It is a bureaucracy—with hierarchical patterns of authority, restricted (celibate male) access to power, ongoing concern for membership and finances, and a vast system of educational, health and social service agencies. These two understandings of the Church—as an intimate group, on the one hand, and as a social organization on the other—are sometimes posed as incompatible. And, incompatible or not, anyone who has remained close to American Catholicism over the past decade knows the bruises that have been sustained on all sides in the controversies over which of these understandings should prevail. Many discussions of parish renewal, for example, include a useful critique of those traditional structures of parish organization that appear inflexible and ineffective. Alternate forms of parish life are proposed, forms which will express and facilitate the local Church's experience of itself as a community. Those who minister in parishes are urged to see community formation as an explicit, perhaps even primary, goal of their work. Often, however, this goal of community can be misinterpreted as the denigration of all organizational elements of parish life, as inimical to the desired development of small, informal groupings of people in which the expressions of mutual concern will be spontaneous and genuine.

A way out of this "small group vs. organization" stand-off may be found in a clarification of the notion of community itself. There are two uses of the term common in current discussion. Often the word is used to indicate a particular quality of interpersonal *experience*. We say "community" when we wish to point to a sense of belonging, an awareness of support, a realization of interdependence, a recognition of shared values, a feeling of communion. But there is another, somewhat different, sense in which the word is used. We say "community" when we wish to designate a particular *social form*, a way in which people are organized or brought together in a manner that will facilitate communication and interaction and thus, it is hoped, lead to the experience of community. Within sociology and social psychology a consensus emerges concerning the characteristics of community as a social form.[3] A better grasp of this sociological understanding of community as a form of group life will enhance ministerial efforts to realize the ideals of the parish as a community of faith.

Community as an Intermediate Style of Social Life

An analytic device used by sociologists to describe the myriad experience of social life is the image of a continuum of forms of group interaction. This continuum extends from the primary group at one pole—a small, cohesive grouping characterized by strong ties and a wide range of shared interests — to, at the other pole, the association — a more formal organization characterized by explicit structures of rights and obligations. On this continuum, community is understood as standing between the more intense social intimacy of the primary group and the partial, more formal organization of the association. Community is a term that refers to ways for people to be together, patterns of group interaction, that fall in the large middle area on the continuum.

The word "community" designates intermediate social forms. A community, then, is both similar to and different from a primary group. And, on the other hand, a community has characteristics that make it both like and different from a formal organization. Current discussion of parish life tends to stress the ways in which communities differ from institutions. For an adequate appreciation of the distinctiveness of community as a social form it is necessary, as well, to note the ways in which communities differ from smaller, more cohesive patterns of primary relationships.

As a social form, community is similar to a primary group in that it is likely that the exchange among members will foster the development of emotional ties. Social cohesion of the group is important for a community. In some ways, the more the members of a community like each other, the better.

But, a community will differ in important ways from the model of the family or other primary group: —in size, in intensity, in diversity.

— —In size. Primary groups must be small enough to allow face-to-face interaction among all members on a regular basis. Membership in a community need not involve each person in face-to-face interaction with all other members.

— —In intensity. The level of emotional exchange and personal sharing that can be sustained in a primary group, due in part to its size, is not a realistic model for personal interaction among all members of a community.

— —In diversity. The size and interpersonal demands of primary groups both require and produce high levels of compatibility, even homogeneity, among group members. Often one of the reasons that a group begins to form — or that people begin to want regular and continuing relationships with each other—is because they recognize similarities. "These people are like me." On the other hand, people who do spend a good deal of time together, who share the same milieu of interests and values, tend to *become* more alike over time. The opportunity for—the pressure for—homogeneity among group members is likely to be greater the more close-knit the group. And consequently, coping with diversity is likely to be a bigger problem. Many groups, on the other hand, seek diversity among their members—diversity of experience, interests, orientation, skills, age or values. A modern university, for example, would be brought to a standstill if homogeneity of skills or interests were a prime consideration in who could work there. In many instances communities, as social forms, require diversity and pluralism to ensure their growth, survival, and effectiveness.

As a social form, community is also similar to an association. It is likely that the focus or concern of a community (more so than in the case of a family or other primary group) will include values or interests that go beyond the group itself. Interaction within a community will usually require more explicit structure, more explicit understanding of the rights and responsibilities of membership, than is the case in a primary group.

But communities also differ in important ways from associations. An individual is involved in a formal organization through a role (e.g., teacher, welder, ticket agent). This role is that aspect of the person's total self which performs the task or service for which the organization was established. The individual's involvement in a community is not limited to just one specialized role. She is known in several aspects of her personality; he is free to be more of himself.

These considerations clarify the sense in which a parish may be said to function as a social form of community. Members of a parish share concern for the religious dimensions of their lives—their experiences of God, of prayer and transcendence, of need and justice, of sin and salvation. This religious concern moves parishioners to come together in various ways—to worship, to share their hopes and doubts of God's movement in their own lives, to plan for the religious education of their children, to act together in the cause of justice and peace. As a community, the parish is like an organization since it involves members in goals and activities that reach beyond their intimate circle of family and close friends. The parish has a mission. Its task is to nourish its own religious life in order that it may act beyond itself, in word and in deed, to witness to the saving presence of God in the world. Some of its activities will be structured and routine, in committees, councils, boards, agencies. Such organization is not undertaken for its own sake, but in order that the religious purposes of the parish may be served more efficiently and effectively. To be sure, parish organization—like organization in business and elsewhere— seems sometimes to complicate rather than to serve the larger goals of the group. But a parish community without any organizational elements would be deprived of an important foundation for its communication and growth.

But the parish community also differs from an organization. An individual's involvement in the parish need not be limited to one specialized organizational role. "More" of the person can come into play. A parish is similar to a primary group since it allows and even expects personal involvement and commitment among its members. But a parish community as a whole also differs from a primary group. Its larger size, its necessary structures of communication and responsibility, its ongoing concern for a mission that includes, but goes beyond, the maintenance and social cohesion of the group itself—these essential elements of parish life make many characteristics of primary relationships inappropriate as goals of a parish community. A parish community should, perhaps, be made up of a number of closely-knit smaller (primary) groupings—families, neighborhood clusters, prayer groups. But the level of friendship within these small groups will be different from the communication that can go on among members of the parish as a whole.

Community is Not a Univocal Term

There is not one social form of community—there are many. There is not one way to bring people together, one pattern for organizing their interaction with each other, one best structure to guide their communication, one model that can guarantee success. Some effective communities will look a good deal like primary groups, with serious attention given to the group itself and high expectations of sharing and mutual support. Other effective communities will function more as organizations, with greater focus on a goal or task outside the group and more limited expectations of emotional exchange. A style of community interaction and definition appropriate as the ideal of community interaction within a prayer group of six or eight people would, most likely, be inappropriate as the definition of what should go on among members of a parish school faculty who wish to make their interaction more communal.

It is likely that a flourishing parish, especially a large urban or suburban parish, will have within it a wide range of group styles—primary groups, intermediate communities, and more task-oriented organizations—each serving a different need within the religious life of the parish, each an appropriate style of interaction for religious people within the Catholic Church. There is sometimes the tendency, perhaps even the temptation, among religious people to think of community exclusively in its primary group connotation. But surely the Christian witness of working together unceasingly—even if not always easily—to hasten the coming of the Kingdom stands equal to the Christian witness of the love we bear one another as a sign to the world of God's presence among us.

Characteristics of Community as a Social Form

There is a basis for community whenever a number of people find they share a concern for some significant aspect of their lives. If this common interest is important enough, it will move them to find opportunities to come together—to discuss, to plan, to act in common in light of the concerns they share. Community is begun in this context of communication and commitment to common goals. But it cannot long persist without an active appreciation for diversity within the group and a willingness to face and resolve the conflicts inevitable in any sustained human relationship.

Within the sociological discussion there emerge five characteristics of groups that function as communities. As a social form, a community is a group characterized by:

1. A common orientation toward some significant aspect of life.
2. Some agreement about values.
3. A commitment to common goals.
4. Opportunities for personal exchange.
5. Agreed-upon definitions of what is expected of membership in this group.

1. Community involves a common orientation toward some significant aspect of life. Community as a social form of ongoing human interaction does not happen, or cannot be sustained, over trivialities. Community occurs around matters of import. Since there are crucial differences among people in regard to what is important to them, it is useful to recognize that people are likely to be moved toward community on the basis of a variety of different issues. What is important enough to one person to provide enthusiasm and energy to work out the many complications of being together over time with a group of other persons may not be nearly so important to someone else. There are many persons in our parishes and neighborhoods for whom their religious faith is of such significance in their lives that it may well serve as a focus of community for them. God, Jesus Christ, the Spirit, Christianity, the Church—these terms and others (perhaps better ones) name aspects of life that matter. A challenge of our ministries within the local church is to work creatively to facilitate the formation and nourishment of communities of faith among such parishioners.

But there are many people in our nation—and a good number in our parishes as they are currently constituted—for whom religion is not an important enough aspect of their lives for it to serve as a realistic focus of community for them at this time. This comment can, of course, lead into a much larger discussion; what definition of religion is being used? should religious faith, however defined, offer the possibility of community for most people? Whose responsibility is it if it does? If it does not? These questions, though significant, are not to the point of the discussion here. One reason it is difficult to build communities of faith in our parishes may well be due to factors of size or distance, or the complexities of modern life. But another reason may be that parish ministers have inappropriate expectations that faith or (probably more accurately in this context) that regular participation in the activities and programs of the local church should be of centrally compelling interest for large numbers of our fellow citizens. This simply is not the case.

But there are other facets of life which might serve as bases for community. For example, questions of child-bearing and child-rearing are, for many couples today, issues of great significance. Whether to have a child, if so, what patterns of love and discipline, of presence and absence, of "mothering" and "fathering" should be developed? Couples and, increasingly, single parents face these questions as issues of personal choice. Many such parents seek, or would respond well to, opportunities to share their concerns, to discuss the dilemmas and delights of parenting that they experience, to discover and weigh—in an atmosphere of support and accountability—the options that are open to them. A group of these adults formed around a common orientation or shared concern for parenting would be likely to develop toward a social form of community.

There are other aspects of life that may serve some among us as the focus of community—interest in the arts, commitment to social justice, appreciation of one's cultural heritage, concern for nature and the environment. Not all these concerns would provide a basis of community for everyone. It is that which is of significance to one's own life that can function as the foundation upon which to base one's efforts to participate communally with others. Not all these concerns would lead, necessarily or explicitly, to the formation of a community of faith. But, efforts at religious community that are not grounded in issues of vital personal significance to the members will be short-lived and superficial.

2. This discussion of the importance to community formation of a common orientation or shared perspective leads to a second characteristic of those groups which are more likely to function as communities. Among members of a community *some* agreement about values is likely—even necessary. It is often not enough that

there be agreement that, for example, parents play a critical role in the development of their children. Those who are diametrically opposed in regard to how parents should undertake to play that role, in regard to which values should predominate (whether, for example, "children should be seen but not heard" or "children should be treated as equals in the family"), are not likely to function well together in a group organized around the values of parenting. They may, of course, work together quite well in some other group. In a group concerned with the preservation of a common ethnic heritage, for example, they may find their values are more complementary.

A community, then, is a group characterized by some *agreement* (but only *some* agreement) about values. As a social form, community need not require identity or conformity on value questions. In a group that is functioning communally there is likely to be a good deal of overlap or congruence on values. Members of a community are likely to evaluate issues, especially issues that are central to the original purpose or ongoing focus of the group, in similar fashion. But the overlap will not be complete coincidence. There will remain areas, even areas of importance, regarding which group members will differ. The challenge of the group's endurance will be its ability to accept and harmonize these differences in ways that contribute to, rather than detract from, the group's effective functioning.

The relevance of this issue of value congruence to the development of the parish community is clear. It is commonplace to acknowledge that the Church is in a time of staggering cultural transition which has resulted in wide divisions within a previously more obviously unified body of Catholic believers. For a parish to function communally there must be a sense that there are broad areas of congruence among members concerning the basic values of their religious experience. There are parishes today in which such a sense of congruence is lacking, parishes that seem polarized over questions of religious values and practice. Efforts to move these parishes toward the experience of themselves as a community of faith must involve explicit attention to this value gap. However, an approach which starts in the attempt to mask differences ("we are really all saying the same thing") or to legislate the end of polarization through enforced uniformity (either "liberal" or "conservative") is likely to miscarry. It is true that in many instances the value disagreements may be more apparent than real, more semantic than substantial. It is true that the minister may be called upon to take a stand in the controversy. But more central in the healing of the parish is the attitude toward diversity and conflict that its leaders display. A parish's ability to move through its polarization toward a more mature expression of its shared belief will in many instances depend upon an experience of reconciliation. Ministers who manifest an appreciation of the range of values within the parish, and a patient confidence in the larger unity in which this value diversity is situated, model an attitude that contributes to such reconciliation.

3. A related third characteristic of groups that function as social forms of community is a commitment to common goals. Communities, more than primary groups, usually include a focus of concern that goes beyond the group itself. There is likely to be, within groups that function communally, an interest in—even an enthusiasm for—action that flows from the members' common orientation and expresses their shared values. Members of communities are drawn to act together in the pursuit of those goals and ideals they share.

The parish is a community for action. Persons come together in the parish in order to accomplish, in ways they could not alone, their goals of worship and service. If it becomes difficult or impossible to accomplish one's religious purposes in the parish—if, for example, parish organizations seem too outmoded to serve as the vehicle of one's religious commitment to justice, or recent liturgical changes seem too great to permit one's expression of worship—commitment to membership and to participation in the parish can be undermined seriously. A parish community is not likely to develop without significant common goals; it is not likely to endure without effective common action.

Common orientation, congruent values, shared goals—there is an important intellectual quality to these facets of the phenomenon of community. These characteristics remind us that community involves knowledge as well as love. Community invites its participants to shared activities of evaluation and planning as well as common actions of acceptance and support.

4. A fourth characteristic of groups which are communities is

the opportunity for personal exchange at a meaningful level. This characteristic would seem to point to the necessity to build into the pattern of group interaction—at least for those groups that would be communities for their members—opportunities for members to communicate with each other at a personal level and to share expressions of mutual concern and care. There is a wide range of ways in which this can be done. Many church people still bear the scars of the experiments in the encounter group model of personal sharing that characterized some efforts over the past decade to overcome impersonalism in church institutions. Many now judge that the usefulness of this model is more limited than some of its early enthusiasts suggested. But there are many ways in which the gift of personal concern is offered and received. The challenge to ministers of a Christian community is to be sensitive to one's people and then creative in devising—or, more properly, in supporting—the expressions of personal sharing and concern appropriate to each group.

5. A final characteristic of groups which are communities is agreed-upon definitions and shared expectations about the group. This involves (1) common understandings of the roles and responsibilities that an individual assumes by becoming a member of this community, as well as (2) common understandings of how the various roles and responsibilities in the group are related to each other.

Each of the five characteristics of community discussed here is an important, even essential, ingredient of any group interaction that aspires to facilitate the experience of community among its members. But in the experience of many in ministry, it is the problems regarding mutual expectations that are the obstacles on which efforts to live together in community most often founder. Each of us carries, perhaps only implicitly, our own definitions or descriptions of an active parishioner, a good priest, a successful parish council, a dedicated religious, a good parish team. These descriptions function as ideal types, providing the criteria against which we will evaluate the actual parishioners, priests, parish councils, religious men and women, and parish teams whom we experience. Complications can arise when persons set about to live together, to work together, to share their experience of faith— each with slightly differing images and ideals of sharing, of cooperation, of authority, of leadership. The diversity in itself is not the problem. As has been suggested earlier, diversity—within certain wide margins—is a potential resource for community. The problem, often, is that these differences are not acknowledged and appreciated.

But the differences do not, for that fact, go away. Often they remain just below the surface—until such time as they erupt, now not as negotiable or even useful differences, but as irresolvable points of divergence and conflict.

This discussion of the structure of community as a social form has returned often to the theme of diversity and pluralism. Pluralism, it has been maintained, can be an important resource for community. But it can be experienced, as well, as a source of complication and as a cause of confusion. The realization of this ambiguous function of diversity in the life of communities calls for a further comment on the ministry of clarification. The effort at clarification is a tool for the formation of a community of faith. The ministry of clarification within community can take several forms. First there is the necessity to make explicit the "oughts" and "shoulds" that are used to evaluate oneself and others in community. Often these criteria upon which judgments are based remain implicit, not fully available to oneself or to others. This is not to suggest that these implicit personal standards are invalid. It is rather to note that when these criteria remain implicit and solely personal, misunderstanding and frustration frequently result.

Next, the process of clarification is important, both initially and periodically, in the life of a community. Those groups are to be commended who devote time during the initial formative stages of their life together to discussion of the hopes and intentions of their members, the roles and responsibilities that each will undertake, the patterns of authority and communication that shall prevail. But change and development are as much a factor of group experience as of personal life. Unless the process of clarification is continued, regularly or periodically, it is difficult to remain alert to the changing images, expectations and needs that occur in the life of a community.

Finally, parish ministers can set out—even rather systematically—to acquire for themselves and to encourage among others in the parish the requisite skills of life in community.

Communication skills are needed—the ability to listen with accuracy and empathy to others; the ability to disclose information about oneself, one's needs, expectations, definitions of community—neither apologetically nor aggressively, but assertively. Skills of conflict resolution, negotiation, problem solving are essential to the effective incorporation of diversity within community. Skills of empathy and imagination enable us to dream beyond the problem that seems to separate us, to a new solution in which we can stand together. And special skills are necessary for the celebration of both our diversity and our community.

These tools of community—skills of clarification, negotiation, imagination, celebration—are clearly not the whole story, especially when we speak of the building up of the community of faith. But skills can form an important chapter in the story of community, a chapter which is, perhaps, too often overlooked.

A further note on the relationship of conflict to community may be of value here. Conflict is one of the inevitable elements of normal human exchange. Whenever persons encounter each other over a period of time, especially if matters of some importance are involved, one can anticipate that differences will be noted, disagreements will develop, discord will emerge. Communities, as social forms, engage members at the level of their significant concerns and are characterized by plurality as well as unity. Conflict is a normal, expectable occurence in the life of such communities.

This is not to say that conflict is a goal of community interaction. But it is to suggest that conflict is one of the dynamics of community life about which our rhetoric is misleading. When we speak about community it is most often upon the experiences of harmony and cooperation that we dwell. Our focus upon these positive aspects is understandable, even fitting. But it can be misleading—leaving the impression that other, emotionally negative experiences of group life are inappropriate to community. Disagreements, anger and competition are standard forces in communal life. The challenge to community is not to do away with conflict among its members nor, worse yet, to refuse to admit or to recognize that contentions occur. The challenge is, rather, to develop ways in which members can deal with the conflicts which will, expectably, develop within the group. A group will not be in existence long before some dissention will begin to be experienced. If the members feel that such contention within the group is, in itself, *wrong,* then it is likely that they will respond to this conflict by avoidance (refusing to acknowledge that some problem exists) or withdrawal ("leaving" the group, physically or psychologically). Neither of these responses contributes to the maintenance of the group.

If a group—a community—is to flourish beyond the enthusiasm of its initial formation, it is important that there be developed among its members *first,* a sense of the appropriateness, or at least the inevitability, of conflict, and *second,* a common understanding of how such conflict can be usefully managed within the group. The methods developed for conflict management can do more than forestall the disintegration of the group. They can be, as well, channels through which the rich diversity of the members is brought to awareness, and, ultimately, put to the service of the community.

The Parish as Community

This vision of the parish as community emerges from our sociological analysis. The parish is the local body of believers whose religious hope is manifest in their ministries of service and sacrament. The parish most appropriately develops the social forms of community, since its goals include both an internal and an external focus. The parish is meant to nourish and express the communion that exists among its members. But this is a communion in meaning and in mission as well as in fellowship. The experience of communion results from, and is sustained by, an awareness of shared meaning and a participation in the shared mission. The mission of the parish has a focus beyond the parish. The parish participates in the task of the whole Church—to witness to the world the saving presence of God among us. The parish can provide a social setting beyond the immediate family, in which individuals experience themselves and are experienced more completely and authentically, apart from the sometimes restricting prescriptions of their particular social roles. Within a parish which is functioning as a community, members will feel free to express themselves more fully, to be present with each other both emotionally and intellectually. Participation in such a parish will invite members to recognize a wider, more public sector of their lives. It will involve them in significant exchange with persons who are not members of their small circle of intimates. The parish which is a social form of community will provide opportunities for individuals to move beyond the psychological and social limitations implicit in one's private life into a manageable, intermediate arena of public life. For many, participation in a parish community can provide a larger social context to assist them in mediating among the claims of the conflicting value systems in which they are immersed through their daily life and work. In the religious community of the parish the individual can be reinforced in the struggle to establish and to maintain a sense of priorities which reflects one's religious commitment. The parish can serve as a context for personal integration, supporting the development of a life-style in which one's deepest values can be shared with others and expressed in common action. The parish is thus a social network in which individuals are challenged to personal conversion (values) and sustained in their attempts to live out the implications of this conversion (action). Personal transformation is the source from which committed religious action, or ministry, will flow.[4]

In the end, the formation of the community of faith remains the work of the Spirit. A well structured group, clear in its goals, open in its communication, committed to its religious values, may still founder. Life remains that ambiguous; faith, that much a mystery. But the minister who is aware of the social dynamics of group life and sensitive to the persons and particular history of *this* parish can contribute importantly to the possibility of community. And the possibility of community is the hope in which we stand, awaiting the gracious visitation of our God.

NOTES

1. For a recent discussion of the possible contribution of the Church as a mediating structure in the American democracy, see Peter I. Berger

and Richard J. Neuhaus, *To Empower People: The Role of Mediating Structures in Public Policy* (Washington, D.C.: American Enterprise Institute, 1977).

2. See Philip Slater, *The Pursuit of Loneliness: American Culture at the Breaking Point* (Boston: Beacon Press, 1970).

3. Those interested in pursuing further the sociological understanding of community should consult: Jacqueline Scherer, *Contemporary Community: Sociological Illusion or Reality?* (London: Tavistock, 1972); E. Digby Baltzell (ed.), *The Search for Community in Modern America* (New York: Harper and Row, 1968); Jesse Bernard, *The Sociology of Community* (Glenview, Il.: Scott, Foresman, 1973); Robert Nesbit, *The Quest for Community* (New York: Oxford Univ. Press, 1970). Also of interest are: Richard Plant, *Community and Ideology* (London: Routledge and Kegan Paul, 1974) and Seymour Sarason, *The Psychological Sense of Community* (San Francisco: Jossey-Bass, 1974).

4. For further discussion of the relationship between community and conversion, see Rosemary Haughton, *The Transformation of Man* (New York: Paulist Press, 1967).

The Religious Mission of the Parish

John Shea

In the course of a recent conference on parish ministry, members of a parish staff outlined their communications network. It was vast in scope, intricate in design, with every possible systems failure anticipated. They showed how their communications network made their programs successful and, in turn, how their programs strengthened their communications network. At the end of the presentation the first question from the group was, "So what? What is the purpose of all this?"

At issue here is the religious mission of the parish. It seems that structures and programs only become meaningful when set within a framework of ultimate purpose. When this framework is not explicitly present, programs and structures seem aimless, vast outputs of energy without a dominant direction. When the ultimate purpose is clear and convincing, the programs and structures which embody that purpose seem meaningful and important. The religious mission of the parish is its underlying rationale, the fundamental identity which informs and guides all its activity.

This question of the religious mission of the parish can be ignored but not escaped. In *How the Church Can Minister to the World Without Losing Itself* Langdon Gilkey notes that the local Protestant churches are very much at home with operational language.[1] What shape is the church plant in? How many people participate in Sunday Service? How much do they contribute? These are typical of the questions which are easily handled at staff meetings. But, religious language which carries the ultimate identity and mission of the local congregation is rarely used, and when it is, it seems awkward and out of place. But, even in these instances, when religious language is avoided, or used in a superficial way, some ultimate purpose of the local church is assumed in all its endeavors. Every concrete practice, from budgeting to programs to personnel, betrays a self-understanding. If the question of mission is not answered explicitly, it is assumed implicitly. Most often it is "under the table," influential in analysis and decisions but not available to be explored and evaluated. At one time or another in most staff meetings it becomes strikingly clear that disagreements on procedures and programs can be traced to varying ecclesiologies. What you think the local church is, determines not only whether certain activities should be undertaken (e.g., should the parish be involved in the busing problem?) but how they should be undertaken (what strategies are consistent with the Christian perspective?). If you belong to a local church, the question is not *whether* you have an ecclesiology but *what* is your ecclesiology.

To explore the religious mission of the local church is a complicated project. Theologically the identity of the Church cannot be approached directly. Church is a derived reality. It was Ambrose who compared the Church to the moon which has no light of its own but reflects the rays of the sun. The Church in itself has no radiance but reflects the light of Christ. More recent appropriations of this insight are J. Peter Schineller's remark, "The function and mission of the Church follows from the function and mission of Christ,"[2] and Jürgen Moltmann's shorthand definition of Church, "ubi Christus, ibi ecclesia."[3] But even this does not fully express the context of Church. Jesus is proclaimed Christ because of his relationship with God. The Church is a reality which comes to be in relationship to the reality of God mediated through the event of Jesus the Christ. Out of this full understanding of Church flows the tasks of ministry. The religious mission of the local Church must be stated in theological, christological, and ministerial terms.

The interrelatedness of theology, christology, ecclesiology, and ministry can be considered from both historical and experiential viewpoints. Historically, the main concern and overriding vision of Jesus was the Kingdom of God. His attitudes and behaviors stemmed directly from his understanding of and contact with the divine activity in human life. The Church, while assuming the Kingdom of God, directed its energies and thought to the person of Jesus Christ. In the standardized language, the proclaimer became the one proclaimed, the witness to faith became the ground of faith. Ministry, while assuming the Kingdom of God and Jesus Christ, focused on the needs of the Church community. What specific tasks must be done within the people of God so that the people may maintain their identity and mission? From an historical perspective the life-giving ecology of Church is God, Christ, and ministry.

Experience uncovers these same connections. If you ask a question about ministry, you are soon dealing with ecclesiology. The nature and function of ministry depends on the nature and function of Church. But any discussion of Church soon leads to its Head, Lord, and Founder. For the Church to be Church, it must be animated by the spirit of Jesus. But to talk of Jesus without talking about God is, quite simply, not to talk about Jesus.[4] The touchstone for questions about ministry is eventually the reality and nature of God. And the converse is also true. Talk of God soon leads to a discussion of the person and event which Christians believe is revelatory of God. But to talk of Jesus and the meanings, attitudes, and behaviors, which allegiance to him suggest, is to be in the process of Church. This Church, the community of the followers of Jesus, naturally inquires about their mission in the world and the ministerial tasks that are necessary to accomplish this mission. If the source of ministry is eventually God, belief in God eventuates in ministry. The linkage is logically tight. To enter the discussion of theology-christology-ecclesiology-ministry at any point means that all points must be considered.

This paper enters that discussion through the category of Church. It stands in the ecclesiological position. Within this position its interest is not the Church on the universal, national, or diocesan level but the parish community. From this vantage point it attempts to sketch a theology, christology, and ministry which will comprise the self-understanding of the local church. The effort is not to state *the* religious mission of the parish but to outline one formulation which is consistent with the Catholic Christian tradition, and meaningfully related to the actual lives of people.

Any understanding of the religious mission of the parish must be concrete enough to be helpful in creating the structures and programs which are necessary for community living. It might be speculatively rewarding to fashion a theology which focuses on universal history, a christology which centers on the hypostatic union, an ecclesiology which is a forerunner of the Parousia, and a ministry which emphasizes authority and untroubled uniformity. But when the controlling perspective is the actual community of believers, a more immediately relatable vision must be constructed. In other words, out of the many approaches to God, Christ, Church, and ministry one must be selected that genuinely and directly speaks to the personal and communal situations that characterize parish life. This formulation becomes a "working ecclesiology." This "working ecclesiology" must be in dialogue with larger speculative efforts so that it does not stagnate and become inbred. But the first task is to formulate and work out of a religious mission which enters into and reconfigures the self-understanding of the actual believing community. Until this happens and happens effectively, there is no common ground for dialogue with alternate theologies, christologies, ecclesiologies, and ministries.

The religious mission of the parish might be characterized as providing the resources and structures for the ongoing interrelating of personal and communal stories with the larger Christian story, for the purposes of redemption.[5] In order to fully understand this mission it is necessary to explore the theology and christology which inform it, and the ministry which is its catalyst, facilitator, and resource. But before this is done, a brief example of this interrelating process from another tradition might help clarify the mission.

One of the most eloquent examples of the interlacing of personal life and traditional story is Elie Wiesel. His most recent work, *Messengers of God* is a retelling of the traditional Old Testament stories in the light of his own experience, and a reappropriation of his own experience in the light of the traditional stories. His telling of the Isaac story is a case in point. Isaac, like Wiesel himself, is a survivor of a holocaust. God ordered his slaughter, then relented. Yet the name Isaac means laughter. The story of Isaac is a tale of the affirmation of life in the face of the despair and nihilism of holocaust. As Wiesel tells the story, his own story is taken up and moved beyond madness and murder.

Why was the most tragic of our ancestors named Isaac, a name which evokes and signifies laughter? Here is why. As the first survivor, he had to teach us, the future survivors of Jewish history, that it is possible to suffer and despair an entire lifetime and still not give up the art of laughter.

Isaac, of course, never freed himself from the traumatizing scene that violated his youth; the holocaust had marked him and continued to haunt him forever. Yet he remained capable of laughter. And in spite of everything he did laugh.[6]

As in any genuine dialogue, both the community's inherited story and the person's own story are transformed in the mutual process of listening and speaking.

It is important to note that the interrelating of personal and communal stories with the Story the community holds sacred is not an intellectual exercise. The purpose is not to match the tales neatly, nor to prove the Bible relevant. The relating is for the purposes of redemption. In other words, this is a process which affirms our created goodness, heals our brokenness, and appeals to our possibilities. The redemptive significance of story is delightfully captured in a Hassidic tale passed on by Martin Buber.

My grandfather was paralyzed. Once he was asked to tell a story about his teacher and he told how the holy Baal Shem Tov used to jump and dance when he was praying. My grandfather stood up while he was telling the story and the story carried him away so much that he had to jump and dance to show how the master had done it. From that moment, he was healed. This is how stories ought to be told.

The story of Elie Wiesel is a single example. Most people in the United States do not have so shattering a story to tell and so remarkable a journey to share. Also Wiesel's is an individual accounting. It does not try to tell how an entire community interrelates with its inherited tradition. But what is important is the process. In dialogue with the symbols and stories that our tradition values as bearers of the sacred, our personal and communal lives are taken up, reconfigured, and given a direction. Vatican II insisted "the parish exists solely for the good of souls."[7] This is one way to understand that declaration.

A Theology for the Religious Mission of the Parish

A theology related to parish life will not direct attention (to use traditional distinctions) to God as he is in himself. This approach often isolates God in a transcendent realm. It imagines a supreme being over against the human person and details his attributes. In this imaginative framework God tends to be distant, contacting the human person only through special interventions or officially recognized channels. But what is needed in a parish environment is a perspective which emphasizes the ongoing interpenetration of people and the reality of God. The focus must be on the movement of God in people, and the movement of people in God. A workable understanding of divine activity in human life is the beginning of the religious mission of the parish.

There are many renditions of how God acts in human life. The most prevalent understandings are the monarchial, deistic, dialogic, intentional, and process models.[8] Although these models are different in content and scope, they are formally the same. They are logical abstractions. They conceive of God and world as discrete entities and proceed to speculate on how they could interrelate without compromising their distinctive features. What results is an intelligible construction without immediate existential import. Only with difficulty and heightened ambiguity can concrete historical events be cited as evidence of God's monarchial, deistic, dialogical, intentional, or processive activity. After David Griffin elaborates a coherent account of revelation using the process model he notes its limits, "The issue here is not, of course, whether these conditions could be verified, but only whether an intelligible conceptualization of an affirmation that might be believed is possible."[9] The models help untangle the mental processes but the naming of divine activity in a particular concrete event is still elusive. Because of this their applicability to a parish environment is limited.

The thought of James Mackay does not put forward another model of divine-human interaction but offers a fresh approach to the symbol "God acts."[10] For Mackay, the traditional contrasting of faith and reason is wrongheaded. In fact this "pitting against" has possibly done more harm to religious people than repressive ecclesiastical structures and obsolete liturgical practices. It implies that faith is not reasonable and that it is in some way outside the realm of the human spirit. Mackay argues that faith must be granted equal citizenship in the city of the human. Faith is one of the ways the human spirit relates to reality, and reality to the human spirit. It stands side by side with science, art, and morality and cannot be reduced to any of them. Although these various approaches are interrelated, they are internally autonomous. Faith is a natural and irreducible human enterprise.

Faith is the acknowledgment of a Creative Will, in and behind empirical reality. This acknowledgment is provoked by the inner dynamics of creaturely existence.

> I became aware that I and my world exist, miraculously exist. They do not found this existence themselves, and they cannot guarantee it. I am unexpectedly alive: always threatened with non-existence, yet positively, at first inexplicably existing. Within that awareness, whether it be an unreflective awareness of my own, or one very much explicated for me by the reflective analysis of a Tillich, lies for me the possibility, my possibility of acknowledging a creative will on which my life depends.[11]

Another approach is to realize that life, the very contingency we are, is an invitation which we may either accept or refuse. "In the last analysis the difference here is not between responding to an invitation or not, it is the difference between seeing existence, life as an invitation and seeing it as absurd, offensive to the human mind."[12] An existence which is given, but not guaranteed, is a sustained invitation.

Although the acknowledgment of a Creative Will reflects the Catholic sensibilities of a natural theology, it is not a proof of God. We cannot disengage ourselves from existence in order to approach it neutrally. In this dimension of human experience the "step back" trick of the mind is misleading. The word is not *knowledge,* the result of objective data and impersonal evidence, but *acknowledge,* the result of address and response. Acknowledgement moves beyond accurate information to entail the relational feelings of hope, love, and trust. In Mackay's thought this acknowledgment is prior to, and the real grounding for, any "proof of God."

> They [proofs of God] are, rather, reflective presentations of a spontaneous, prereflective insight or conviction of the human spirit that—involved in this contingent existence—however the contingency is felt in the concrete; in change, birth and death, order and the breakdown of order—there is a Creative Will. [13]

Faith is the word for the human spirit's natural acknowledgment of God.

The person who relates to reality through faith encounters events and people which startle, deepen, and reconfigure his faith. When this occurs, the religious person often uses revelational language to uncover its deepest meaning. The person does not say, "I believe God is active here." Instead he moves to the divine point of view and says, "God is active here." Although this move adds nothing new to the experience of religious faith, it is both necessary and appropriate. Only revelational language expresses the intensity of the faith conviction. It is a natural transition within the language of faith.

> If I acknowledge God, the creative will both beyond and in the universe, both transcendent and immanent, that very acknowledgment naturally translates itself into affirmations that God is active in this historical world, particularly in its key events, more particularly still in those events which have significance for the future of religious belief, most particularly

of all in the people at the centre of such events, the people whose events, in a very real sense, they are. The moment the language of faith (that is, language which involves the characteristic words of that category of psychic behaviour, such as acknowledge, belief etc.), translates, as it naturally does, into the language of affirmation, one finds oneself speaking from God's point of view, and very shortly after that one is into the category of revelation.[14]

Also the foundational concern of the religious person is to lead his life in the light of his faith conviction. He wishes to understand God's intention so that he can commit himself to God's future. Revelational language performs this expressive and concrete task.

Mackay's revolutionary understanding of divine activity seems a rich and versatile approach to the parish environment. Mackay has reversed the revelation-faith procedure. God reveals himself, the traditional order asserts, and then we respond in faith. In this understanding, energy is focused on finding genuinely disclosive events and protecting them from the infringement of psychology, science, and history. Is God acting here or is it only man and how do we tell the difference? In Mackay's scheme, to talk about divine activity is not to hunt for supernatural input or to detect "something extra" in the situation. Language about God's activity discloses the significance of those encounters which have inspired us "to believe, or to believe once again, or to believe with a new intensity or a new direction in life."[15] Therefore the religious mission of parish begins with those experiences which function to stimulate the life of faith.

In the life of each individual, and in the life of each community certain experiences are paradigmatic. In the self-understanding of the person, paradigmatic experiences do not function as one more incident but "give a pattern" to what went before and what comes after. They are significant moments or encounters or time-spans when a life is reconfigured or the journey takes a new direction. If this reconfiguration is in an outward and open direction, bringing health to the individual and the community, we speak of God's redemptive presence to that life. Although the experiences that function as faith-renewing are unique to each individual, there are some common and recurring themes. The boundaries of life, the experience of wonder at birth and the experience of anxiety at death, invite people to renew their stances in relationship to the mystery within which they find themselves. The experience of love, desiring the well-being and the presence of another; the experience of moral ambiguity, trapped in the awareness that the good I would I do not, and the evil I would not that I do; the experience of injustice, angry at oppression and striving to create structures of justice; the experience of commitment, standing for a conviction and value in an ambiguous world; the experience of belonging, of sharing fundamental hopes and fears. All these experiences, and many more, have triggered a faith appropriation of human life. When a parish gathers around these experiences, it gathers around the activity of God.

A Christology for the Religious Mission of the Parish

It is not enough merely to gather around those experiences which trigger in us a faith appropriation of our lives. Those experiences call for interpretation. Explicit religious symbolization mines the richness of the experience and so enables us to relate to the full meaning of what was encountered. One approach to christology is to understand it as the way Christians symbolize and interpret the divine activity in human life. In other words, talk about Jesus is Christian code for talking about the religious meaning of contemporary experience. This approach to christology can be divided into (1) retelling the story of Jesus and (2) relating the Christian symbol system (of which the symbol of Christ is the focal center) to the concrete experiences and ongoing stories of individuals and groups. In both ways the goal is to use the inherited Christian tradition to articulate and seize the present activity of God.

Retelling the story of Jesus in such a way that God's present activity is brought to consciousness is grounded in the Christian belief that God and humankind have met and mingled in Jesus of Nazareth. And so a shorthand way of talking about both God and the human person is to tell a story about Jesus. The stories of Jesus have a triple focus. They are about God and humankind filtered through Jesus. In philosophic and sacramental theology the mediatorship of Jesus Christ has been thoroughly explored. But it has not always been recognized that the Gospel portraits of Jesus can also be understood in terms of mediation.

There is a way in which the stories of Jesus are not about Jesus. It seems that during his lifetime Jesus resisted questions about his personal identity. He deflected them toward the central motif of his preaching—the Kingdom of God and the radical demands it makes on human living. Therefore, attempts to uncover what Jesus thought of himself must go the way of indirection. For example: if, as some exegetes contend, the context for the parable of the laborers in the vineyard is that Jesus was being attacked for his attitude toward tax gatherers and sinners, it is startling that he responds by telling a story of how God acts. It is argued that this certainly reveals something about how Jesus conceived of his relationship to God. "There is a tremendous personal claim involved in the fact that Jesus answered an attack upon his conduct with a parable concerned with what *God* does!"[16] Although Jesus' response might betray his awareness of who he was, it is preeminently another example of how Jesus redirected questions to the God-person relationship.

It is often said that the early church did not display the same hesitancy about Jesus as he himself did. The focus shifted from the God-person relationship to the identity and work of Jesus. Although this is undoubtedly true, there is an alternate perspective on the relationship of Jesus and the early church. This perspective is reflected in the conclusions of redaction criticism. The evangelist was not a neutral collector and arranger of Jesus material. He had points to make and Jesus was one of the ways he made them. To some extent the Jesus who emerges in each Gospel carries the theological agenda of the writer. Therefore it is necessary to talk about a Matthaen, Markan, Lukan, and Johannine Christ.

The evangelist tells the story of Jesus so that God's present activity within the community is focused. The emphasis is on the present revelation and the story of Jesus is reconfigured to speak to that situation. So, for the persecuted, yet hopeful community of

Mark, Jesus is the suffering Son of Man who will return on the clouds. For the community of Luke who must learn to live in history, the apocalyptic portrait of Jesus is modified. Jesus becomes the exemplar of Christian life. The difference between Jesus and the believer is downplayed. The same Spirit which animated Jesus animates the believer. Like the believer, Jesus prays and attends worship; like Jesus the believer forgives his enemies (Stephen). In this perspective christology does not investigate the psychic make-up of Jesus but uncovers how the story of Jesus symbolizes the historical relationship of God and his people.

This way of doing christology seems especially suited to the parish environment. Within any parish many stories of Jesus are continually being told and interrelated. Different groups restructure the raw data of the gospels so that a particular image of Jesus emerges. One group strongly stresses Jesus as a man of prayer and appropriates all other stories about Jesus through that filter. Another group emphasizes Jesus, the man of compassion; another Jesus, the friend of the oppressed and the fighter for justice; another Jesus, the man for others. The danger involved in multiple Jesuses has been continuously and legitimately stressed. But in this christological approach they do not represent naive retrojections or a lack of respect for historical accuracy. A parish as a whole and groups within the parish continue the evangelistic traditions. They do not tell the stories of Jesus out of historical motives but out of religious instincts. The stories of Jesus which they tell direct them to those dimensions of their lives where the reality of God is active and calling. The people who tell the stories of Jesus cited above find God in prayer, compassion, social justice, and service. In this way they are connecting their personal and communal stories to the archetypal story of the Christian tradition.

The second way of doing christology so that the divine activity is highlighted is to interrelate present experience and Christian religious symbols. This way is more direct because the personal and communal stories are explored on their own terms before they are brought to the story of Jesus. It is also more flexible because it explicitly employs the whole constellation of Christian religious symbols. In other words, our personal and communal stories are interpreted through the symbols of God, Christ, Spirit, exodus, covenant, judgment, kingdom, creation, fall, incarnation, atonement, crucifixion, church, eucharist, heaven, hell, sin, grace, etc. This relating process creates a Christian consciousness which suggests certain attitudes and encourages certain behaviors.

A concrete way in which symbol and experience interrelate can be outlined in four stages. (The chart on the following page develops a few examples through the four stages.) The first stage is an exploration of the personal and communal stories. In the chart these spaces are blank because each story is unique. Each has its own feeling tone, its own angle of vision, its own importance in the full biography of the person or group. Although each story is indisputably singular, certain patterns emerge. Willa Cather once remarked: "There are only two or three human stories, and they go on repeating themselves as fiercely as if they had never happened." The story is dense, ambiguous, multi-directional. The pattern is general, clear, and focused.

The pattern does not attempt to capture the riches of the story but selects from among the riches a dominant concern, something "core" enough to function as a controlling perspective. In order to relate experience effectively to a religious symbol it is necessary to grasp the pattern which is present yet hidden in the story. To move from story to symbol without the mediation through pattern often leads to a sense of unreality. The symbol floats above the story, never really making contact and so never really having impact. In the first stage the story must be thoroughly explored; in the second stage the pattern must be clearly stated.

An example: when her mother finally succumbed after a long illness, Clare experienced loss and loneliness. She had expected that. What she had not expected was the powerful urge to take stock. Her mother's death occasioned a careful scrutiny of who she was and what she was doing. She became aware of her own contingency in a heightened way, a way that was influential for decision making and behavior. She wondered about the life she found herself within and the responsibility she had to it. Clare's story continues and is as complex and multi-dimensional as Clare herself. One pattern that emerges from her story is that she is becoming aware of an inescapable relatedness to mystery. Her mother's death is pushing her to ask what meaning she assigns to

STORY	PATTERN	SYMBOL	INTERPRETATION
	inescapable relatedness to Mystery	God	acceptance, critique, call (Abba)
	brokenness, alienation, death-dealing	Sin	idolatry, ultimate allegiance to what is finite
	wholeness, belonging, life-giving	Redemption	enlargement of life, reestablishing creaturehood
	person or event crucial to well-being	Grace	gift that strengthens and inspires
	supported and challenged by the story of Jesus	Gospel	find, sell, buy (the dynamic of the parable of the Kingdom)
	supported and challenged by another	Spirit of Christ	sacramentality of grace
	sense of hopefulness beyond suffering and evil	Heaven	fidelity of God
	sense of peril, the dangers of freedom	Hell	dualism, universalism, annihilation
	human solidarity and the cry for justice	Kingdom	God's future as permanent critique
	the acceptance of life, celebration, affirmation	Eucharist	community response to Mystery in the memory

life and how she should live. This generalized pattern, among others present in her story, can lead to a Christian religious understanding of her life.

The pattern which crystalizes the story is the key to which religious symbol (stage three) should be pursued. Patterns reflect the continuing situations and themes of the human condition. These perennial situations are the experiential home of religious symbols. Sin relates to our experiences of brokenness, redemption to our experiences of wholeness, and grace to our experiences of people and events which are crucial to our well-being. But to match symbol and pattern is not sufficient. In Ricoeur's catch-phrase, "The symbol gives rise to thought." An interpretation (stage four) of the symbol is necessary if the story is to be illuminated and critiqued. Since many interpretations are possible, one must be chosen which we will "speak" to the story. The dynamic of the process moves from stage one to four and from four back to one. The actual story suggests the pattern, symbol, and interpretation. In turn, once the interpretation is developed, it moves through the symbol and pattern to reconfigure the story. The influences in relating personal experience and Christian religious symbols are continual and mutual.

The example continues: Clare's realization that she is in an existence that is given but not guaranteed is the traditional experiential locus for the symbol of God. In other words, from a Christian perspective the transcendent meaning of the Mystery to which she is inescapably related is God. One interpretation of this Mystery is Jesus' designation—Abba. The Mystery within which she finds herself is intimately related to her and accepts her unconditionally. This unconditional acceptance does not lead to complacency, but highlights those areas in which she has not responded to that acceptance. This critique is not arbitrary condemnation but an essential element in the call to new life. If Clare allows this religious-theological interpretation entry into her story, she will be appropriating her life from a Christian perspective.

What happens in the relating process is that consciousness is structured, attitudes are formed, and general behaviors outlined. In short, the interaction of symbol and experience creates world. Within this world certain attitudes are encouraged and others discouraged. In the world of acceptance, critique, and call structured by the symbol of God and the interpretation of Abba, the attitudes of self-hatred, pride, and sloth are alien. What is encouraged is a stance of fundamental acceptance which is open to a process of growth characterized by critique and call. The relating process suggests a broad directionality for behavior but does not supply a guide to the complexities of concrete situations. To move within the symbol of Abba suggests a lifestyle of love but does not assure the ability to love or the knowledge of what the "loving thing" is to do in any situation. The religious mission of the parish is the ambitious task of formulating and living out of a Christian perspective.[17]

A Ministry for the Religious Mission of the Parish

The religious mission of the parish is not a separate activity. Within the life of a parish there is not an isolated endeavor known as Christian storytelling which stands over against liturgy, religious education, social services, social change, and administration. The religious mission of the parish is a dimension of all its activity. The storytelling process goes on through liturgical, educational, social service, social change, and administrative activity. The religious mission is not one thing the parish does but the permeating context of all it does.

The storytelling process is the ongoing atmosphere of all projects and the vocation of all the members of the local church. Ministry to this process insures that there are structures and resources for the interrelating to go on and that the conclusions of the process are embodied in effective personal and communal programs. *De jure*, this task belongs to the priest whose role designation is to unravel the meanings and behaviors which our relationship to the sacred suggests. *De facto,* this task falls to whoever is capable of doing it.

Since the religious mission of the parish is operative in all its programs, part of the training of ministers for liturgical, educational, social, and administrative tasks will be the ability to be a catalyst, facilitator, and resource for the storytelling process.[18] This means a triple stance for the minister in relation to the people. (It is extremely important for the minister to know at any given time which stance he is adopting.) He initiates the type of question or perception which will lead to a faith appropriation of the situation. He helps the people hear and clearly articulate the religious, theological, and ecclesiological dimension of their situation and programs. He becomes a theological resource, relating the contemporary situation to Christian perspectives and values.

In order to empower the ongoing process of religious mission the minister must possess helping and change-agent skills. The minister must be able to quiet his own agenda and help the person or group explore their story. If the minister is not able to help on this basic human level, the stories are never fully told and the interrelating remains shallow. Also, the minister must know the principles of effective programing. The result of the interrelating process is usually strategies for personal and social change. If the minister has change-agent skills, he can be a resource to the implementation of the new self-understanding the relating process occasioned. Since the environment of the parish is people and programs, helping and change-agent skills are the presuppositions of effective ministry.

The most important skill of the minister vis-a-vis the religious mission is the theological ability. The minister must be able both to hear the religious dimension of the human story when it is articulated in secular language and to handle explicitly theological questions. He should be able to surface the religious, theological, and ecclesiological assumptions which dictate people's perceptions and the direction of programs. Finally, he should be able to relate the Christian story to the concrete, everyday activity of the parish.

The major resource for this ability is the Christian tradition. If the minister is to be the central figure in the storytelling process, he must have access to the larger Christian story. Knowledge of Christian scripture and theology is a necessity. This knowledge must not be self-contained data with nowhere to go. It must be knowledge which understands its relation to ongoing life situations and its power to influence decision and action. This knowledge is not vaguely applied or overlaid on the pastoral situation but, through the helping and change-agent abilities, integrated into the lives of people and the systems in which they live.

Someone has suggested that the perennial Christian strategy is: (1) Gather the folks, (2) break the bread, (3) tell the story. This paper has attempted to outline a religious mission of the parish in terms of Christian storytelling. In order to do this it was necessary to sketch a theology and christology which would make this task meaningful, possible, and desirable for a parish community. Also it was necessary to discuss briefly the ministerial skills which would insure that this religious mission can be carried out effectively. The religious mission of the parish is more than a backdrop for endless activity. It is its fundamental identity, the vision which supports and challenges, gives direction and purpose, sustains and renews. Without it, the buildings, people, and programs are another organization; with it, they are a Christian parish.

NOTES

1. Cf. Langdon Gilkey, *How the Church Can Minister to the World Without Losing Itself* (New York: Harper & Row, 1964), pp. 128-146.

2. J. Peter Schineller, "Christ and Church: A Spectrum of Views," *Theological Studies,* Vol. 37, (December, 1976), p. 549.

3. Cf. Jurgen Moltmann, *The Church in the Power of the Spirit* (New York: Harper & Row, 1977), pp. 4-7, 66-132.

4. Cf. Langdon Gilkey, *Naming the Whirlwind: The Renewal of God-Language* (Indianapolis: Bobbs-Merrill, 1969), Part I, Chpt. 5.

5. For an understanding of the larger Christian story cf. John Shea, *Stories of God* (Chicago: Thomas More Press, 1978).

6. Elie Wiesel, *Messengers of God* (New York: Random House, 1976), p. 97.

7. *Christus Dominus: The Decree on the Pastoral Office of Bishops in the Church.* No. 31.

8. Cf. Ian Barbour, *Myths, Models and Paradigms* (New York: Harper & Row, 1974), pp. 155-170.

9. David Griffin, "Is Revelation Coherent?" *Theology Today,* Vol. XXVIII (October, 1971), p. 293.

10. David Mackay, *The Problems of Religious Faith* (Chicago: Franciscan Herald Press, 1972).

11. Ibid., 85.

12. Ibid., 87.

13. Ibid., 95.

14. Ibid., 201.

15. Ibid., 192.

16. E. Linnemann. Quoted in Norman Perrin, *Rediscovering the Teaching of Jesus* (New York: Harper & Row, 1967), p. 118.

17. A contemporary catechism which employs this method of relating human experience and Christian religious symbols and which is extremely useful in a parish environment is Andrew Greeley's *The Great Mysteries* (New York: Seabury Press, 1976).

18. For a fuller treatment of these ministerial skills cf. John Shea, "Doing Ministerial Theology: A Skills Approach," in *Vatican III, The Work That Needs To Be Done* (New York: Seabury Press, 1977).

The Parish:
Ministering Community and
Community of Ministers

Gerard Egan

Introduction

In addressing the notion of ministry in the parish setting I intend to do the following:

—————Point out some differences between organizations and communities in our culture.

—————Develop an expanded notion of ministerial leadership in the faith community.

—————Develop the notion of "ministering congregation" and contrast "lateral" with "vertical" ministry.

—————State some of the essential principles of effective systems.

—————Briefly apply these principles to parish ministry.

I approach the question of parish and ministry from the viewpoint of social and organizational psychology. This does not mean that social and organizational psychology are to replace our religious understanding. It means rather that we take seriously the theological principle that grace builds on nature. If we ignore the principles of effective organization in our attempts to build the Christian community, we do so at our own risk. And it is our ministry that is most likely to suffer.

*Some Differences Between Organizations
and Communities in Our Culture*

Systems, whether organizations (such as General Motors) or communities (such as a neighborhood or a parish), exist to meet human needs and human wants. Organizations meet these needs and wants in at least two different ways. Organizations usually manufacture products (e.g., furniture) or produce services (e.g., hospitals provide medical services) for people outside the system (e.g., General Motors manufactures automobiles for the general consumer market, and it is only incidental that its employees also buy GM automobiles). However, GM, as an employer, also meets the job and career needs and wants of its own employees.

Communities such as parishes, on the other hand, provide opportunities for social living, services, and sometimes products (e.g., a communal farm) for its own members. In organizations the needs of employees can be met only if the system is successful (that is, it makes a reasonable profit) in providing products and services for consumers. Communities, while not organizations, still need to be organized in order to be effective in meeting goals. Therefore, they often have organizational "arms," as it were. For instance, a neighborhood will have a "community council" empowered to help a particular community meet its needs. The council "ministers" to the needs of the community. Both communities and organizations, therefore, need to have a fundamental working knowledge of how to organize and the skills necessary to implement this knowledge. And so, we pose these questions. What are the characteristics of a good organization? Do the principles of good organization apply to communities such as parishes as well as to the organizations of the business world? Let us take a brief look at ministerial leadership before answering these questions.

Leadership in the Parish Community

For the first five decades of this century social scientists studied the traits or personality characteristics of leaders in order to determine the nature of leadership. It is probably fair enough to say that almost every conceivable personality trait has been related at one time or another to leadership behavior, status, or performance. And yet, this trait approach—pursued diligently for a half century—has taught us very little about the nature of leadership, for it concentrated too heavily on the designated leader, ignoring other elements of the leadership process such as the "led" and the situation. This trait approach to leadership has long been abandoned in the research literature, but its myths still haunt us in our educational systems (including the education of ministers). The supposition is that if a person develops the proper traits, he or she will emerge as a leader and by that very fact there will be leadership in the parish community.

But leadership is far more than the designated leader (the "head") or even the "real," though informal, leader. Leadership is a complex interactional process involving the leader or leaders (both formal and informal) together with his or her, or their traits, the "led" and their talents and needs (including how they view and relate to both formal and informal leaders), and the situation (including task, geography, history, and other factors). This system can be depicted by a triangle each of whose sides indicates interaction in two directions.

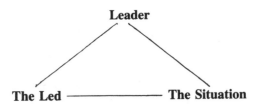

It is this total complex that constitutes leadership. If a community satisfies the needs of its members by achieving clear, behavioral goals through effective programs executed by effective people, then that community is exercising "system" leadership. This is more than just "managerial" leadership and more than the influence of any given leader. "System" leadership is a function of the entire system; all who contribute to the well-being and effective functioning of the community participate in this kind of leadership (which, of its very nature, takes precedence over mere "managerial" leadership).

Such "system" leadership is not simply a fiction invented to provide patronizing social rewards for active community members ("The picnic wouldn't have been the success it was without you, Henry, and the other members of your committee!"). Rather it is a summary of the working together of all the elements that constitute the "logic" of a well designed and well functioning system. This is not to say that "managerial" leadership is not essential to the working of a system. But managerial leadership is only one of the roles called for by the structure (the way work is divided up) of a system. Managerial leadership itself is distorted when it is taken out of the context of the whole system or is seen as the principal or sole cause of a system's effectiveness. Let us begin to apply some of this logic to ministry, especially ministry in a parish.

Ministry

It is possible to draw a parallel between "system" leadership and ministry and between "managerial" leadership and, at least in part, the work of "officially designated ministers" (e.g., the pastor and his associates or the members of the parish ministerial team—those for whom ministry is a career). In this view, ministry is not just what officially designated ministers do but rather a function of the faith community. Ministry in the fullest sense means meeting the pastoral needs of the members of the community ("system" leadership). Therefore, it would seem that one of the most important ministries of officially designated ministers is to facilitate the "doing of ministry" in the congregation. While it is evident that officially designated ministers will themselves minister (e.g., engage in sacramental and other ministries), it seems just as evident that one of the principal tasks of officially designated ministers is to encourage all the members of the community to participate in its ministry.

One way to concretize the term "ministry" is to relate it to the "works of Jesus." By the "works of Jesus," I mean, among others, the kinds of behavior designated under the rubric of the "spiritual and corporal works of mercy." These works may not include all forms of ministry, but they have the advantage of being quite concrete (and concreteness of goals, as we shall see below, is one of the requirements of a well designed and well functioning system).

The Logistic Absurdity

Ministers of all denominations have traditionally involved themselves in what may be called a "logistic absurdity." It is impossible for officially designated ministers to take care of all the pastoral needs of the members of the communities to which they minister. The "works of Jesus" affect all dimensions of the lives of the members of a community of faith. For instance, there is a church-related hospital near Chicago which has 15 full-time and 15 student chaplains, and they are all busy. What are we to say of a hospital that has only one or two chaplains? The pastor who has a hospital in his parish could spend all day every day in the hospital and still not exhaust the possibility for ministry. Research in the helping professions has shown that an increase in the number of professional helpers available to a community is followed by an increase in the number of those seeking help. There is some evidence indicating that an arithmetic increase in the number of helpers is followed by a geometric increase in the numbers of those seeking help. If ministry is defined in terms of the direct delivery of services that meet the pastoral needs of the members of a faith community, when is the work of officially designated ministers done? Ministers are left frustrated or perhaps, paradoxically, consoled by the fact that they have worked hard all day (the 60- or 70-hour ministerial week) and by the fact that the supply of pastoral needs is inexhaustible.

The "Ministering Congregation"

If officially designated ministers are to be more than symbols in a community (that is, symbols of the fact that there *is* One who is defined as Care, even though *de facto* caring does not take place extensively in this world), then the congregations in which they minister and exercise pastoral leadership ("managerial" leadership) must become "ministering congregations," that is, ones in which the members minister extensively to one another. (As an aside, it strikes me as odd that many of us who are grouped together in communities of ministry—rectories, seminaries, convents, campus ministry centers—presume to use these groupings as bases for ministering to others when we find it difficult or impossible to minister to one another—the very thing we are promoting.) In ministry we have, in my opinion, too long been preoccupied with one corner of the leadership triangle, the leader, the officially designated minister exercising managerial leadership and involved in the direct delivery of services. We have not given nearly enough attention, practical or theoretical, to the other two corners—(1) the pastoral needs, the talents and resources, and the possible contributions of the members of the community; plus (2) the variety of works in the variety of situations that constitute ministry. The parish is the interactional matrix where all of these elements are constantly being combined in an effort to achieve "system" leadership, that is, a "ministering congregation." All who in the name of Jesus act in such a way as to meet some portion of the pastoral needs of a community are by that very fact exercising pastoral leadership ("system" leadership). They are doing the works of Jesus. All the members of a community of faith can have the rewarding experience of exercising this kind of leadership.

Lateral Versus Vertical Ministry

When officially designated ministers engage in the direct delivery of ministerial services (e.g., hearing confessions, visiting the sick), this can be called "vertical" ministry. When, on the other hand, the members of a parish community, moved by their own initiative and supported and challenged by officially designated ministers, minister to one another, this can be called "lateral" ministry. When officially designated ministers work to see to it that this kind of initiative is developed among members of the congregation, then they, too, engage in "lateral" ministry.

I believe that lateral ministry is most likely to take place in faith communities that organize themselves according to the principles of effectively designed and functioning systems. When the question—"Why don't we have more ministering congregations?"—is asked, some blame officially designated ministers, while others lay most blame on the members of the congregation. Those that blame the ministers say that ministers have not wanted to share their ministry ("managerial" leadership) with the members of the community. However, many ministers, whether freely or in obedience to a higher command, have made attempts to diffuse their authority. But in the parishes in which authority has been shared (e.g., through the parish council), there is little evidence that there has been a concomitant rise in the level of effective ministry in the community. That is, sharing authority has not been the answer to increased "system" leadership.

Nor does it seem that all the blame belongs to apathetic, reactionary church membership. No one in his or her right mind would deny the fact that there are many apathetic Christians, but there are also a great number of willing Christians who have not tapped their own resources. Perhaps a balanced view would take both ministers and congregations for what they are in the main—*ordinary people.*

Congregations are made up of ordinary people, plus a small percentage of parishioners who are energetic, highly motivated, and eager to participate in the work of the Church.

There are a number of dynamic, creative ministers in the full-time service of the church but most are the "ordinary men" (and the ordinary women) discovered in the study of American Catholic priests (Kennedy and Heckel, 1971).

This is not to belittle either ministers or congregations. Almost a century ago William James suggested that few people use more than a fraction of their potential in facing the tasks of life. Most of us are saddled with a "psychopathology of the average," to use Maslow's (1968) term, so pervasive that it goes unnoticed.

In the last hundred years few have challenged James' observation, just as few have done much about the socio-cultural systems—family and education, especially—whose mission it is to help people develop their potential. Neither ministers nor laity have received or are now receiving the kind of socio-psychological education *and training* needed to develop their own human potential and to help make them successful contributors to the socio-cultural systems, including church, in which their lives are embedded (see Egan and Cowan, 1978).

Education, for the most part, remains overly cognitive in nature and provides little training in such life skills as self-management, interpersonal communication, problem-solving, and program-development. It is true that most of us pick up enough of these skills from experience to survive, but the lack of systematic training in life skills as part of both formal and informal education is one of the reasons why most of us do not actualize more of our potential. "Enough to survive" is equivalent to the "psychopathology of the average."

What this means is that when it comes to organized, systematic approaches to ministry, most of us have a great deal to learn both in terms of working knowledge and skills. Officially designated ministers merely sharing ministry with members of the community is not enough. Lateral ministry needs to take place in the context of a community capable of organizing itself to meet its total pastoral potential.

*The Characteristics of a Well Designed
and Well Functioning System*

A community of people, insofar as it organizes itself to meet its purposes and to provide services for its members, has a need to respect the laws or principles of good organization. In a well designed and well functioning community:

(1.) Members know what human *needs* they are trying to meet through the formation of community (e.g., the need for companionship and intimacy; the need to stay in touch with religious roots and traditions). Therefore, the members know how to assess their needs.

(2.) Members formulate general or wide-ranging statements

of *mission,* the values, theology, and philosophy of the community ("We want to promote the 'works of Jesus' among ourselves, that is, we want to feed our hungry, visit our sick, help the imprisoned").

(3.) Members establish concrete, specific, behavorial, measurable, and attainable *goals* and objectives that are adequate translations of mission statements (e.g., identifying elderly shut-ins needing help; providing such services as transportation, shopping, cleaning for these shut-ins).

(4.) Members design step-by-step *programs* (means) to achieve each goal and objective (ends) (e.g., liturgical services for those interested in communal prayer; study groups for those interested in deepening their awareness of Scripture).

(5.) Members acquire the working *knowledge and skills* needed to execute these programs efficiently and effectively (e.g., a working knowledge about how patients experience being in a hospital and the human relations skills needed for visiting the sick).

(6.) Members see to it that whatever *resources* beyond working knowledge and skill are needed to execute programs are available at the time they are needed (e.g., automobiles to transport shut-ins, meeting rooms for study groups, etc.).

(7.) *Structure.* Members divide up the tasks of the community, including "managerial" or leadership tasks, in ways that best serve the needs of the members and in ways that promote the fullest participation of members (e.g., lay ministers make more frequent communion visits to shut-ins possible).

(8.) *Relationships.* Members have a clear idea of what to expect of themselves in terms of the tasks of the community and of what they might expect of one another (e.g., what to expect from those in "managerial" or leadership positions).

(9.) Members communicate with one another, especially for: (A.) *Information sharing.* Giving and receiving freely whatever information is needed to get the tasks of the community done. (B.) *Feedback.* Giving and receiving recognition for tasks successfully accomplished, and criticism (respectfully and caringly shared) to remedy failures. People in managerial positions are open to receiving feedback of both kinds.

(10.) Members know, understand, respect, and use effectively such *basic principles of human behavior* as reinforcement, modeling, and shaping in pursuing the goals of the community (e.g., members do not expect people to show up at poorly designed and unrewarding liturgical services).

(11.) *Climate.* Members cultivate an open community in which free and informed choice is normative, in which members exercise leadership rather than vie for power, in which conflict is faced openly and without rancor, and in which opinions and proposals affecting the membership, especially the opinions and proposals of those in managerial positions, are presented in such a way as to be open to disconfirmation.

(12.) *Environment.* Members know how this community affects and is affected by other socio-cultural systems in the environment. Members (and perhaps especially those in managerial positions) defend the community from environmental forces that would do it harm and help the community contribute to the growth and development of socio-cultural systems pursuing similar goals (e.g., members take a stand against urban "renewal" that will affect the community in such a way as to benefit the rich and harm the poor. In a more positive vein, members federate with surrounding like-minded communities in order to pursue common purposes more effectively).

This, then, is the "logic" of effective organization. This logic is applied in somewhat different ways to business concerns and to communities. For instance, in communities good relationships are not just a means of getting the work of the system done. Good relationships—people being with people in caring ways—constitute one of the goals of community life and, therefore, programs are developed to promote human relationships. Nevertheless, if communities violate the logic of good organizing, they, like businesses, will suffer because of it. (For a comprehensive review of these principles, see Egan, 1978.)

*Lateral Ministry in the Context
of an Organized Ministering Community*

Now let us review some of these elements of an effectively

designed and functioning system in the light of lateral rather than merely vertical ministry.

Needs. One way of getting a feeling for the logistic absurdity of direct delivery of ministerial services by officially designated ministers is to review what ministers actually do with their time. A composite list describes an enormous number of tasks, each demanding specialized skills: designing and executing tasteful liturgical services, preaching, visiting the sick, budget and other financial tasks, teaching, assessing parish needs, maintaining church property, organizing and running meetings, counseling, running youth programs, helping the elderly, hearing confessions, helping the parish relate to the surrounding community, to other churches, Catholic and non-Catholic, and to the larger polity, social programs, teacher training programs—and the list goes on. Each minister, it is true, carves out his or her own "package" of ministerial tasks depending on how he or she establishes priorities, but the other tasks, often representing important community needs, still remain. Even delimited "packages" require an array of skills that go beyond the resources of many ministers. In a word, the needs of any community are too great to be serviced by a team, much less by one person.

Effective communities are committed to ongoing self-renewal and periodic review of community needs as part of the renewal process. Since systems exist to satisfy needs and wants, ongoing assessment of needs and the ways they are or are not being met is a critical function of a system. The more concretely members define their needs, the more likely will these needs be reflected in the mission statements, goals, and programs of the community. What needs does the parish meet that are not being met through family or neighborhood or government? Or what does the parish, ideally, add to family and civic life? How deeply do people feel the need that parishes are set up to meet? These and similar questions need to be answered so that the members of a community of faith get as concrete an idea as possible of the needs that parish community is established to meet. And in a parish community with a sense of lateral ministry, needs will be assessed through the collaboration of both officially designated ministers and the members of the community themselves.

Mission. Given the richness of the Gospels and of Christian tradition, it is relatively easy for the church to formulate rich statements of mission. This is not the weak link in the organization of parish life. Mission statements that center around helping people constantly rediscover their religious roots, renew the bonds of service and love which, ideally, unite them, and reformulate their hopes for the future are one of the most attractive dimensions of Christian community life. Given the nature of parish life as we know it, one may ask whether these statements of mission promise too much. A more useful criticism might be that mission statements drawn from a rich tradition are not formulated in such a way as to respond to the needs of *these* Christians living in *these* times. For instance, mission statements concerning meeting the liturgical needs of people in the United States should perhaps take into consideration the individualistic, fragmented, and pluralistic character of much of American life.

Goals. Goals are behavioral translations of more general mission statements. While mission statements can be general and wide-ranging, goals must be specific and behavioral. Many systems, especially those involved with human services (e.g., government, education, the helping professions, and, of course, church), find it difficult to spell out clear, behavioral goals. Churches have an added problem. Goals are meaningful only if they are *adequate,* that is, substantial translations of mission statements. Given the richness of our mission statements, the relative poverty of some of our *de facto* goals is disturbing. The "psychopathology of the average" of parish goals and programs stands in stark contrast to the possibilities suggested by the Gospels.

Poverty of behavioral goals that are adequate translations of parish mission statements are understandable, perhaps, in parish systems characterized by merely vertical rather than both vertical and lateral approaches to ministry. After all, officially designated ministers can be expected to bite off only what they can chew, and goals and programs are tailored to the resources of such ministers, no matter how industrious they might be. Community goals and programs that are substantial translations of mission statements of their very nature demand the ministerial participation—including participation in "managerial" leadership—on the part of many church members. In a sense, a parish can afford behavioral clarity of goals only if there are people with the time, energy, and motivation to pursue these goals.

In a well designed and well functioning community, clear and concrete goals are communicated to the members and members are committed to the goals. Member commitment to goals is ensured (1) if members participate in the setting of goals, and (2) these goals touch on real needs. Both of these conditions highlight the importance of lateral ministry in a parish.

The importance of behavioral clarity in goal setting can hardly be overemphasized, even though it is difficult to achieve. All of the other elements in the "logic" of organizing for effectiveness such as program development, education and training, structure, relationships, and communication are affected by the quality of goals. Fuzzy goals lead to fuzzy programs with inconclusive results.

Programs. Programs are means. They make sense insofar as they are developed to achieve clear-cut goals or ends. My fear is that many human services delivery systems, including Church, substitute concrete programs for concrete and clear goals. The execution of program gives the impression of vitality even though these programs do not meet real needs. We see this happening constantly with respect to government-sponsored programs. They are ushered in with great expectations, but eventually they die, sometimes a long, agonizing death, because they do not meet the real needs of the members of the community. Too often parishes sponsor missions, develop adult education programs, stage sports nights, establish committees and clubs, and the like without first determining whether these programs achieve goals that translate mission and respond to real needs. It is true that such programs do bring people together and by that very fact promote some kind of community (part of the mission of church). But programs for the sake of programs are haphazard and run the risk of achieving goals that are inadequate translations of mission and which, therefore, do not contribute much to the life of the community.

Well designed and well functioning communities develop

programs only after needs have been assessed and goals have been established. Programs are added or eliminated on the basis of their contribution to established goals. A parish, in one sense, is a federation of programs which achieve concrete goals that translate mission and meet real needs. The manpower needed to execute these programs comes, of course, from the membership. A parish with a strong sense of lateral ministry will not have problems finding people to implement programs.

Working Knowledge and Skills. Carrying out parish programs demands certain kinds of working knowledge and skills. Goodwill in ministry, whether vertical or lateral, is no substitute for competence. We have long given lip service to the dictum that "grace builds on nature," but in ministry "nature" still receives short shrift. If a parish is to become an effective ministering congregation, then *all* who participate in ministry need to develop, both in themselves and in others, the "nature" on which grace builds. In concrete and practical terms this means, in part, the development of the basic skills of community interaction: (a) the ability to understand others from their frame of reference and the ability to communicate this understanding; (b) the ability to challenge others in ways that promote "standing with" rather than "standing apart"; (c) the ability to contribute to and use the resources of the group.

These and other life skills are essential to intensive community living (whether the "community" is a friendship, a family, or a larger system such as a house, church or a parish). Theoretical knowledge is of less value here than "working knowledge," practical knowledge that results in understanding and leads to action. Paradoxically, the working knowledge and skills needed for effective human and systems involvement are not provided in any systematic way by either formal or informal educational systems. Skills training is practically unheard of in these systems. As I have already noted, the expectation that even moderately high levels of these kinds of working knowledge and skills will be picked up "from experience" is unwarranted. Certainly the levels of working knowledge and skills needed for more intensive community living are not, except in rare cases, picked up through experience.

Perhaps parish communities could themselves become interim education and training centers, providing the kinds of working knowledge of human development and the kinds of skills needed for community living which are not provided by other systems.

Parish communities thrive on volunteer help. But volunteers do not last long in poorly designed systems. We know the signs of such systems.

People refuse to volunteer, not necessarily because they are lazy or uncommitted, but because (a) there are no effectively organized programs for which they can volunteer and/or (b) they do not feel that they have the skills to do anything useful. Ministry, like any other experience, is a rewarding experience only for those who do it well.

People who do volunteer often drop out of programs quickly either because the program is ineffectively designed or because they realize they do not have the skills needed to be effective. Their experience is a painful one and therefore they withdraw. This, too, has nothing to do with apathy or poor motivation.

Some volunteers without the requisite skills stay on and "mess things up." With luck such volunteers are harmless, but there is evidence that they do more harm than good. Programs are effective only if they are staffed with effective people.

This does not mean that parish programs must be staffed with professionals, that is, "credentialed" professionals. There is convincing evidence that many credentialed professionals are not "functional" (effective, skilled) professionals. Volunteers who are trained for specific forms of ministry can become "functional" professionals. In the parish, credentials, including ordination, must be demythologized and put into perspective. The "credentialing" demands of sacramental ministry aside, the quality of ministry is more important than the credentials of the person ministering. It may be that because of our traditions, many people in the parish would prefer credentials (especially ordination) to effectiveness. If so, this is an important area for reeducation.

Structure. Structure refers to the way in which the work of the system is divided up. Structure leads to the various roles and relationships found in a system, including "managerial" leadership roles and the relationships associated with such leadership. In a community of faith, managerial leadership, while important, is not to be overemphasized. Managerial leadership and its authority are to be understood as services to the community and not as symbols of higher status. In a community of faith, structure should promote goals, that is, opportunities for building relationships and the mutual exchange of services. Any monopoly over ministry on the part of officially designated ministers would not only be a logistic absurdity but contravene the very goals of the community. Professional ministers, therefore, have the responsibility of developing the leadership and ministerial capacity of the broader parish community.

Evaluation. I would like to end this brief discussion of some of the critical elements in the logic of the design and functioning of a community with a few words on evaluation. The question of accountability in ministry has been receiving more and more attention recently. Unfortunately, it has been, for the most part, restricted to a consideration of the work of officially designated ministers and to their "managerial" leadership. We cannot have it both ways. We cannot urge parishes to move toward lateral ministry and reserve accountability for officially designated ministers. If lateral ministry is critical for the life of the community, then accountability pertains to the entire life of the community and to all forms of ministry. The community is accountable for the quality of its life. Evaluation pertains to "system" leadership and system effectiveness primarily, and not just to the "managerial" leadership of either officially designated or other ministers.

Evaluation, at its best, is an ongoing process that is part of the natural, day-to-day life of the community rather than some kind of judgment at the end of a program or a process. Evaluation-as-judgment contributes very little to system effectiveness, while ongoing evaluation offers great promise for system self-renewal. Ongoing evaluation makes mid-course corrections possible.

The elements critical to ongoing evaluation are:

(1.) *Clear, behavioral goals.* If goals, subgoals, and objectives are clear, then and only then will it be clear when these goals have been achieved. If "only God knows" whether the community of faith is successful in achieving its purposes or not, this in itself is a sign that it is not. I believe that the greatest obstacle to accountability in the parish is the lack of clear, concrete, behavioral goals communicated to all participating actively in its life.

(2.) *Systematic programs.* If clear, step-by-step programs have been elaborated to achieve behavioral goals, then those responsible for the execution of any given program will be able to tell what progress they are making. If programs are unclear and haphazard, then ongoing evaluation is impossible.

(3.) *Concrete feedback.* Good feedback is short, clear, concrete, and descriptive of behavior rather than evaluative of the person. It includes recognition of what has been done well as well as of what can be improved. It is given as frequently as necessary and as soon as possible after the behavior in question. In a well designed and well functioning system, feedback is given readily and flows in all directions throughout the system. Members do not apologize for either asking for or giving feedback.

There are a number of possible sources of feedback in any given system: oneself, coworkers, persons who receive services, perhaps even supervisors or managers. In a well designed and well functioning system, all sources of feedback are open.

Conclusion

It does little good to encourage lateral ministry in a community if the community as a system is poorly organized. For then the lack of success of lateral ministers will be attributed to the fact that lateral ministry "does not work" instead of to the poor organization of the system itself.

Even though I believe that lateral ministry is no longer a luxury or an option for faith communities, I do not imply that the promotion of lateral ministry is easy. There is understandable resistance from some officially designated ministers, who feel that their status or even their identity is endangered. But beyond that, change in systems of human services does not come about easily. Since the goals of these systems are often fuzzy (even though they are ongoing concrete programs), there are often few clear-cut criteria for success or failure. In fact, these systems go on and on whether they are "successful" or not. After all, even when they are inefficient, they *do* provide *some* services. As a result, those with managerial responsibilities are not under pressure to change.

If the Church is to grow as a significant force in the life of its members, then people must make lateral ministry happen. To paraphrase Kropotkin, ministry, like freedom, cannot be conferred—it must be seized.

BIBLIOGRAPHY

Egan, G.   *The skilled helper: A model for systematic helping and interpersonal relating.* Monterey, CA: Brooks/Cole, 1975.

Egan, G.   *Interpersonal living: A skills/contract approach to human relations training in groups.* Monterey, CA: Brooks/Cole, 1976.

Egan, G.   *Change agent skills: Models for designing and changing systems.* Monterey, CA: Brooks/Cole, in press.

Egan, G. and Cowan, M.   *Human development in human systems: A working model.* Monterey, CA: Brooks/Cole, in press.

Kennedy, E. and Heckler, V. J.   *The Catholic priest in the United States Psychological investigations.* Washington, D.C.: U.S. Catholic Conference, 1971.

Maslow, A. H.   *Toward a psychology of being.* Second edition. New York: Van Nostrand Reinhold, 1968.

The Parish as Locus
of Liturgical Ministries

Daniel P. Coughlin

Mary Gillian has just read over the passage *Isaiah 56:1-7* for the fifth time. It used to be the difficult words that would bother her. Now she wrestles more with meaning. She sometimes wonders why such a passage as *Isaiah 56:1-7* is selected for such a beautiful summer day as today. Sometimes she wishes she understood more about Scripture. Her twelve years of parochial education do not always seem to help. Sometimes she wonders if her children will understand the meaning of the Scriptural words she will be reading at the 11:00 a.m. Mass at St. Joseph's parish. Always she wonders how Father Granowski will shape his homily to give contemporary meaning to her reading. The Sundays she is a lector are different Sundays. Not only does it mean her husband Jim helps a bit more to get the children ready for Mass while she practices. The Mass itself means more to her when she has a part in it.

Jim Campello has just picked up the coffee pot and poured himself a second cup of his favorite wake-up elixir. Holding the Sunday morning paper in his other hand, he is caught somewhere between a stretch to the kitchen cabinet and the table, suspended between the quiet of his aloneness at the breakfast table and the violence of the front-page news.

He picks up a piece of toast and at the same time, looks at his watch. Only thirty-five minutes until Mass begins. He looks at his hand and the bread, and reflects a moment on the importance of food and feeding. His gesture of giving as a minister of Communion has caused him to think more about the many hungers of mankind, the openness demanded of all humble enough to receive from others. Lately, his gestures of self-giving have confronted his own lack of generosity. It is almost time to leave.

Not since he was ordained a deacon, not since he started to bring Communion to the sick at Browning's Nursing Home on Sunday mornings two months ago has Bob Ewing felt prepared for Sunday Eucharist. Once again, today, he is standing leaning on the vestment case only twenty minutes before Mass is to begin, writing some introductory notes for the penitential rite and the gesture of peace. He always tells himself this is a simple enough task, but he never seems satisfied or prepared. He sincerely wants to help the people pray the Mass. It isn't that he is nervous anymore, being up in the Sanctuary. No. That never bothered him. He just simply wants to do a better job. It is only a few words. But he wants his remarks to the congregation during the celebration of the Eucharist to be reverent and understandable, simple and sincere. He doesn't want to be just a "potted plant" or a distraction up there in the Sanctuary to the people. At the same time, he wants the entire community to share with him the vision and the joy of their lives as it has come to him since as a deacon he has been touching the sick, listening to the brokenhearted, encouraging the young and congratulating the old. He wants his friends in the parish and even those he doesn't know too well to see in him, a symbol of their own lives.

Father Granowski has been a pastor for only three years. He finds his parish a challenge and a great joy. From the young associate pastor and the rest of the staff, to the janitor and the kid who sells newspapers in front of Church on Sunday, he is grateful to them all for what they do for him, for each other. Without everyone's contribution, each doing his/her job, well and conscientiously, he would not have nearly as much to be grateful for as he celebrates the Eucharist, with them and for them.

He worked hard on this homily. But even while he is vesting, he is hoping, wondering, praying that what he has to say will really speak to them—to their hearts. He is really coming to love these people. He hopes his words will touch their lives. He prays that the words of the Church's prayer will be strong and direct enough to embody the pain and happiness he sees on their faces and hears them talk about. He wants so much that this Eucharist will be seen as theirs. Not his prayer, theirs. A celebration not of his ministry, but theirs, simultaneously—serving and being served—jointly celebrating their relationship one to another. One in Christ.

In every parish the Sunday Eucharist is the celebration of multiple ministries, converging at a given point in time to the praise and glory of the name of Jesus. Liturgy does not exist in a vacuum. Jesus and all wise theologians since him have cautioned that liturgy is not an end in itself. Persons were not made to find a place and role in a divinely dictated liturgy. Rather, it is the other way around. A true and good liturgy manifests the reality of parish or community life. If there is little ministry, weak community and a paucity of talent in the parish, this will show at Sunday Eucharist. Any liturgical moment is honest and authentic, insofar as it manifests the authenticity of Christian service and gospel values, or it does not. Liturgies cannot be criticized for producing poor communities if the climate for, and experience of, the registered parishioners is already poor community.

A liturgy cannot create fictitious reality for them, because then their worship would become idolatry, their prayer a blasphemy. A community's liturgy will reveal exactly what is going on in its midst—nothing more and nothing less. Hopefully, every liturgy thereby truly reveals Christ, forming and reforming his people. Quite unaware at times, the community has not realized the power and presence of its salvation. Often, individuals, as well as the community as a whole, have not recognized Christ as this power in its midst. The drama of individual lives and community events has not been integrated into a paschal mystery pattern or enlightened enough by faith to enable one to see the Spirit at work.

Every liturgical celebration gathers the best that a community has to offer to the Lord in praise and the best that can be offered to others by servicing each other's needs. Any liturgy that pretends to be more than what the community is or hopes to be is fictitious and deserves the condemnation of false gods. Liturgical celebrations, for this reason, are risky because they demand radical honesty, sincere commitment and genuine service. If mistrust, division or manipulation of peoples exists in a community, it will show itself when the community is gathered for liturgy. At the same time, if liturgical celebrations reflect more than actuality, or the passing moment as a finality, liturgy appeals to the deepest aspirations of mankind yet unattained. Honest prayer manifests what people desire for themselves and for the world. For this reason alone, liturgies are necessary for communities. Liturgy enables us to see ourselves at our best. Because liturgical celebrations capture the utter authenticity of our character, and try to put our failures and successes into an honest context, liturgies are frightening; while a liturgical celebration that does not reveal the complexity of personal and community life is a sham.

Any parish is a network of relationships. Those personal and group relationships can be based on personal gifts and peer support as well as communal concerns and group motivation. A liturgy can solidify all these strengths. Each parish has a history that is only as old as its living memory and each parish has hopes and aspirations that are only as real as the sweat and toil they engender in the lives of individuals. A liturgy of Word and Sacrament quickens the memory and stirs the spirit. The liturgical ministries provide the community with sustenance at this level of existence. Week by week, people mature in each other's dreams and associations, memories and hopes, meaning and significance, human importance and communal solidarity.

When a parish gathers to pray, and thereby express its deepest conflicts, its strongest hopes and its proudest moments, it is presumed that its liturgy will be revealing. A liturgy should reveal what is going on and what is not going on in parish life. If visions, hopes and perspectives are narrow and constrained, that will show in the way people pray or desire to express themselves to God. If visions and dreams are not passing fancies but energizing realities that inspire the young and maintain the old, design reforms and frame the daily work of the people, then the liturgy is approaching its fulfillment. Never an end in itself, the liturgy of a parish does not celebrate "where the community is at." Rather, a true liturgy helps people express where they *realistically* hope they could be. Liturgies not only demonstrate people willing to serve the community by the liturgical roles they perform. Liturgies challenge, motivate, refine and activate people for social ministry.

Liturgical celebrations are to be comprised of people who are unafraid to express their hopes and their sorrows. Always a present moment, a liturgy brings people back to their past and makes them deal with the unfinished business of unrealized hopes and unfaithful promises. It also makes people look starkly and boldly into the future. Only radical believers can hope for a new world and a new day when dreams and aspirations will be fulfilled, especially if they are honest enough to admit that what is going on now does at times diminish hope of a better tomorrow. A sound and true liturgy will help a community sort out its honest aspirations from its passing fancies.

Because the parishes we live in are so different from those we theologize about, it is important to realize that a parish liturgy helps us to be in contact with the needs and gifts of people about us. Our honest needs for security or belonging, for trust and acceptance as well as for challenge and motivation must be met in some way or other. If the family unit cannot appreciate the depth of these needs and respond to them, then the extended family or community will try. Every parish with diverse peoples and diverse needs will try in various and creative ways to respond to the needs of its people. Its liturgy will manifest this effort, not only in its prayers where hopes and aspirations are aired, but in its ministries, which symbolize the totality of the celebrating community.

Every parish liturgy should be evidence of the ministerial nature of the local parish. Lectors, ministers of communion, ushers, parish musicians, deacons, priests and those behind the scenes, such as artists, planners, sacristans, graphic designers and printers, are all part of the parish liturgy. More importantly, each personally, and together as a unit, they manifest the ministerial nature of the local parish community.

Everyone who participates in the liturgy has a role. Even the most passive participant standing against the exit doors in the rear has a contribution to make. Ministry is always a personal contribution, investment or participation in an entity larger than oneself. Every participant contributes to the whole, the total effect of its worship, and its service in ministry.

Because the liturgy is a communal prayer, comprised of individual expressions and personal revelations of faith, every liturgy manifests, at one and the same time, the sameness of its unifying power and the pluriformity of creative expressions of this power. Each person must be sincerely, unobtrusively and unhesitatingly present to the Lord and to one another. At the liturgy, there can be no hiding, no shielding or evasion and no withdrawal. It is incumbent upon every member of the community to reflect upon his or her gift. Whether the gift be small, such as reading, silent prayer or troublesome questioning, or large in sincerity, talent or artistry, it makes no difference. If the whole community is denied even the smallest contribution or slightest enlightenment, all are less for it, all are left in a greater degree of poverty and darkness. When gifts are denied within self and not shared, they are denied to all.

Because the parish is a unique microcosm of Church, and a cross section of myriad and multiple relationships, it has an immense possibility of uncovering and developing these gifts in people.

When gifts of persons are recognized, affirmed and celebrated in community, as in a liturgical celebration, the gifts can no longer be denied. Even if the person chooses to deny the existence of the gift in self, the community will not allow it. When a community gathers to pray, its richness in diverse gifts and various expressions is proclaimed to a world which, left to itself, might not only deny the gift, but even the need for the gift.

More and more parishes are recognizing that there are certain people who have special gifts, unique and appreciated, that enrich the community. At Eucharist especially, although true of all sacramental moments, these gifts become apparent. The community gathered for prayer sees itself mirrored in the liturgical ministers gathered in the sanctuary. The liturgical roles symbolize and personalize the gifts to be found in the community's people.

Liturgical ministries are not designed simply to make the task of the priest easier or less. Liturgical ministries, rooted in baptism and confirmation, are the right and responsibility of all. It is primarily the plentitude of talent and numbers that enables communities to choose certain persons to perform particular liturgical roles. Although some are ordained for full-time and constant ministry and thereby have defined liturgical roles, others are not ordained and can perform various liturgical functions depending on personal talent, the need or the occasion. In any given parish, the ordained and the unordained, salaried and volunteer ministries must coexist, correlate and coordinate with each other so that all may be one in rendering fitting praise to the glory and power of Christ, who is active in all and has drawn all together to acknowledge and proclaim him as Lord.

Although the pastor himself might well, at least figuratively, be the best coordinator of the various ministries, sometimes this coordination can best be managed by a committee or liturgical team. Liturgical teams have grown through recent years. They have not grown in size and number as much as they have grown in wisdom by their pastoral practice. At one time, liturgy teams were identified with planning particular or weekly liturgies. More likely today, a liturgy team is a helpful and often necessary way of coordinating the various existent and emerging liturgical ministries in a parish. People serve the Lord and each other as lectors, ministers of music, ministers of communion, acolytes, ushers or welcomers, artists, planners, hospitality, bakers, dancers, presenters of gifts, singers, cantors, leaders of prayer, commentators, deacons, priests and as bishops. Persons who assume these roles must do so with humility, grateful for their gifts and willing to share these gifts with their brothers and sisters, not to their own praise, but only to the glory and praise of the Lord Jesus. No matter what their role, if this internal disposition is not present, it will show and mitigate the effective prayerfulness of the liturgy.

Persons who have liturgical roles are not only in need of coordination, so that the gifts complement and augment each other and in this way build up the Body of Christ, they are also in constant need of formation. Their gifts must be shaped by practice, understanding and proper direction until they flourish into liturgical art forms, resplendent with nuance, charisma and grace that speak of human grandeur. Training sessions and disciplined practices will help people perform their best for the dignity of divine worship. Such training should never lead to pretense or

"showyness." Instead, the personal characteristics of each minister must be so shaped and encouraged to develop, that the benefit
of personal competence, assuredness and quality, once achieved,
is preserved and perpetuated for the good of the whole community. Spiritual formation is equally important, for the internal
dynamics are the wellspring from which true liturgical ministry
should draw. There is no substitute for personal prayer, and
abnegation to release integrity and freedom. When personal talents are rooted in these gifts of the Spirit, great light can be gifted
to the people of God. Personal presence must be taken seriously
and gospel values must be lived. Then, the transparency of self
will elucidate the undeniable strength and power of Christ, living
in the very midst of his people.

In every parish, those responsible for getting people involved, for directing and managing their liturgical expertise and
overseeing the various ministries, must make it their constant
endeavor to construct ongoing or at least occasional formation
programs. Parish liturgical ministers should operate on a regular
cycle of introductory formation followed by a formal presentation
to the community, regular pastoral service, a time of review and
reflection, continued or advanced formation sessions, a liturgical
commissioning ceremony, and so on. Persons should serve in
liturgical roles until their service is no longer life-giving and
spirit-enriching for them personally or for the community. A rota-
tion system, whereby a large percentage of parishioners have the
occasion of serving in some liturgical way, is most ideal. The
constant freshness and creativity of the Spirit can best be realized
when new people and new roles and new interpretation of those
roles is continually unearthed.

When a parish gathers to pray, it reaches beyond the present
dimension and tries to make unrealized hopes more tangible. As a
locus for liturgical ministries, every parish has the potential for
enabling its people to grow spiritually, assume responsibility and
begin to serve others and grasp the concept and experience of
ministry.

Because of their liturgical positions, Mary and Joe gain a new
perspective on the Church, their community and themselves.
Mary realizes a power within herself she never realized before.

Joe is becoming more reflective. The consequences of his faith on his values and life-style have been more apparent since he has taken on a public role in the liturgy. Bob is discovering that public worship is enabling him to assume more and more responsibilities in the community, without fear, hesitation and apologies.

Priests like Father Granowski, gathered for the Eucharist, are becoming more and more aware of the community context in which sacraments are celebrated. He is inspired himself and rejoices in what he sees happening in people around him. At least, when he stands at the altar these days, he sees the semblance of a ministering community. Who knows what the consequences of such a Eucharist will mean? It is already changing people. It may change the Church. And someday, maybe even the world. Until that total transformation into a new creation takes place, there will be people gathering daily and weekly in their parish churches, tending the dream of such fulfillment. These ministers, by careful use of their gifts, will keep the story of salvation alive, they will inspire hope and confirm belief that Christ will win out in the end. By reading, movement and song, they will instill this vision in others like themselves. These liturgical ministers will pray and lead others to prayer. Every Sunday, their gathering will celebrate their presence, their desire to serve and their unique and very personal contributions.

As they try to get inside the prayer of Christ and make it their own, as they lift the prayer of the Church from the page and bring it to life in themselves and reveal it to others, something will be occurring. As they give their all, their best, to the Lord and to the congregation, it will be Christ empowering them. It will be Christ at work in his people, shaping and forming, challenging and encouraging, confronting and consoling, until they all become one under his power. Until all are ministered to and until the needs of ministry are all fulfilled, people will gather, ministers will surface, and Christ will be celebrated.

The Parish as Source of Community and Identity

Philip J. Murnion

"Community" and "identity" are slippery notions, hard to grasp with any assurance that we have them well in hand. And it may appear to some that by spending any time on these notions we are encouraging a kind of indulgent introspection that is more harmful than helpful. It is true that preoccupation with community and identity can immobilize us and keep us from "getting the job done," especially if we approach these concerns with the view that we have to "get our act together" before we can do anything worthwhile. In fact, however, there are ample grounds for asserting that both community and identity are problematic in today's society and today's Church. But we may be able to identify ways in which the resolution of both problems will occur in action, rather than as a pre-condition for action.

There is considerable evidence of the problem of community and identity. A person's identity is tied up with his/her roles, with the need to fulfill the ongoing expectations of others. And there are few roles where the expectations are not changing. It is much harder now to be confident about what it means to be a man or a woman, a husband or a wife, a parent or a child; or, in Church life, a priest, a lay person, a religious. The great popularity of Gail Sheehy's *Passages*[1] is but the most recent reflection of the mid-life confusion people are experiencing concerning their relationships, their careers, and their life projects.

If secure identity is problematic for many, so is community. For, if my identity involves the roles I have, it then involves the relationships I have. And there is considerable evidence of breakdown in these enduring, anchoring relationships we call community. The fragility of family relationships is evident both in the climbing divorce rate and in the growing reluctance of young people to enter into the commitment of marriage. Erosion in Church community is reflected in extensive disaffiliation from most churches. Scepticism about the national community is evidenced in declines in both voting rates and party affiliation. And loss of a civil community is testified to by rising crime rates and by the decline of neighborhoods. Whatever cultural currents converged at that time, disintegration of these communities simultaneously accelerated in the late sixties.[2]

Problems of identity and problems of community are real enough and are shared by every segment of society, rich and poor, secular and religious. It may help us in our efforts at renewal of parish life to reflect on some aspects of these factors as they are experienced in Church life. We will do this by (a) considering the nature of the Church as a symbolic value community; (b) reviewing what it was that made the Church community of the past such a strong community; (c) acknowledging some of the new conditions that affect any attempt to restore the Church community; (d) surveying current efforts to revalidate the Church community; and (e) pointing some areas where further development seems necessary.

Church as a Symbolic Value Community

A deservedly popular book is Avery Dulles' *Models of the Church,* in which he sketches the essential features of five current approaches to Church life. The assumption behind the book is that the Church as a community of faith can take many forms, none of which fully expresses all the dimensions of the Church's life. The fullness of the life of the Church constantly eludes our attempts to capture it in statement, in relationships or in action. I suggest that we reflect on this quality of the Church, not as a source of frustration but as a feature of the Church community that we must always preserve. It may help us to appreciate this feature of the Church by considering the Church as a symbolic value community. Let me explain.

In a sense, all communities are value communities and it is this that distinguishes them from other groups whose bonds are some ad hoc shared self-interest. These interest groups I call coalitions. A community, on the contrary, is constituted by the relationships among people who are committed to certain values. These include the value of each member, as a person, to the other members, the value of sustained commitment to one another, and values that members share as foundational to their identity. Other values to consider are ways the members approach life and death, individual freedom and collective responsibility, person, family, work and material reality. Some such values are freedom, justice, development, solidarity, mutual responsibility and the like. Also included will be the meaning we assign to power, to success or failure, to poverty or wealth. Are power and wealth significant in themselves or are they only significant or legitimate to the extent they are used in service to others? What are the realms of freedom and when must freedom be curtailed in favor of community values and equality? These are value questions.

Formal communities may articulate their values in constitutional statements about rights and their protection. Informal communities generally express their values in their behavior; their work, their ceremonies, whom and what they honor.

The Church is such a value community, a group that does more than serve my immediate needs, a group that shares, supports, and clarifies the values that are most foundational to my life.

The Church is also a symbolic community, that is, it is a community that (a) expresses some meaning for life; (b) engages more than the intellect; and (c) moves us to action which is expressive of the deepest elements of our being. For this is what a symbol entails and the Church community must stand as a symbol of the Kingdom of God in the world. Values and symbols share three dimensions that must be present in the Church community and activity at every level. These three dimensions may best be expressed by the following definition of "value":

A value is a conception, explicit or implicit, distinctive of an individual or characteristic of a group, of the desirable which influences the selection from available modes, means and ends of action.[3]

A value (and a symbol) involves a conceptual or cognitive aspect, an expression or affective aspect (the desirable), and a motivational or ageric aspect. It embraces a way of thinking about something, appeals to the affective or esthetic dimension of our being, and moves us to action. Both the value and the symbol are never fully expressed or realized. They are part of a world we are constantly attempting to experience more fully.

Any attempt at Church community must take these dimensions of a symbolic value community into account. On the contrary, attempts at Church community that neglect these components are necessarily defective. What are some examples of such defective attempts? One example is an approach to liturgy that simply attempts to appeal to passing sentiments, however intense for the moment, or to a desire for communion, without suggesting or expressing the relationship between these feelings and more transcendant elements of faith. These liturgies can be so preoccupied with what is immediate to our experience that they are really quite trivial. A different kind of neglect may be found in liturgy or religious education that simply appeals to the intellect without either providing for the affective side of human commitment, or moving people to more authentic Christian action. There are many other examples of approaches to Church community that do not reflect the nature of the community as a symbolic value community. Some of these will be pointed out below, but anyone in pastoral ministry can reflect on the degree to which this ministry provides meaning, commitment and motivation to action.

Now, let us look back at the past form of Church as one example from which we can extract the critical elements of Church community.

A Comprehensive Community

Recollection of the Church community of the past can evoke either nostalgia or anger, and usually for the same reasons. The Church community of the past, largely embodied in the parish but with important broader dimensions, was a *comprehensive* community.[4] It is not surprising that Catholics who feel only too keenly the absence of secure community recall with fondness a past situation where there was a clear order to the universe and to life and where it was clear what it meant to be Catholic. (Even many non-Catholics express dismay about the disintegration of that community.) But it is also understandable that many Catholics recall the past Church community as stifling to the intellectual and emotional expression of the individual. For there was a comprehensive order to the community, but this order could also be experienced as extensive constraint on the individual's thinking and behavior. This relatively closed community fostered extraordinary *solidarity* in the face of its enemies, which were seen to be the "international conspiracy" of atheistic Communism and the domestic hostility of Protestant America.

Whatever one's reaction, nostalgic, rebellious, or even realistic about the fact that the Church of one time will not be appropriate to another time, it will be helpful to identify critical ingredients of that community.

The Church community of the past, composed predominantly of poor immigrants from rural areas, provided an impressive array of mechanisms for supporting and empowering this minority community. Theology offered *meaning* to the whole of life and death and *clear rules* governed almost all of life, public and private. The very *naming* of a child had to link the child with the communion of saints. Baptism in which the child was specially *garbed* in white, not only freed the child from original sin but introduced the child into a pervasive process of socialization and a life of grace channeled to the Catholic by the priests and rites of the Church. Names, titles and special garb would mark further expressions of deepening commitment and responsibility (first communion, confirmation, entrance into the religious life, priesthood, episcopacy, and papacy), critical moments of life (marriage and funerals), and admission to an elite (monsignors, knights and ladies).

From within the resources and institutions of the Church were provided as many *necessary services* as possible: education, health care, child care, financial relief and counselling, as well as recreational opportunities for children and adults. This was possible because of the great *sacrifices* made by parishioners for the good of all, for the works of the Church.

Time itself was given special meaning. More than half the days of the year had some religious significance. Sundays, holy days, Lent, Advent, every Friday, special local feasts, Saturdays and eves of holy days and first Fridays when confessions were heard; all provided religious significance to the temporal framework of life. Many of these observances (going to church, fasting and abstaining, wearing ashes) also involved *public witness* to one's identity as a Catholic. *Space* was likewise shaped, geography into dioceses and parishes, private homes into sacred places marked by crucifixes and sacred images, and special places such as churches or religious houses with their still more reserved sanctuaries and cloisters.

There was a special *language,* not only the Latin of the liturgy, but words Catholics used: sacrament, confession, merit, grace, absolution, and others. We had our own *music* and our own *signs;* we signed ourselves with the sign of the cross, used holy water, genuflected, wore ashes and crucifixes and medals. Our school children wore uniforms.

And we were likely to call the priest even before the doctor when death struck ("I am a Catholic. In case of accident, please call a priest").

To the many expressions of local parish identity were added expressions of *national* and *universal Catholic identity*; processions honoring national or town patrons and patronesses, ceremonies and collections for the missions, a calendar of saints from across time and space, many references to the Pope and his picture displayed not only in church buildings but even in many homes.

Time, space, language, music, diet, names, the sacralization of every key moment in life, comprehensive meaning and rules, provision of essential services, common enemies of a people in a shared lower class status, sacrificial investment in the care and development of all Catholics, a missionary sense, sanction for failure and forums for forgiveness, the mediating of grace through the sacraments and structures of the Church, all made the Church community most significant. Such an enclosed community is no longer possible, whether it is desirable or not. Nonetheless, we can distill from this experience the critical elements of such a community.[5] They are the following.

1. *Providing a meaning-context for life that relates immediate experience to transcendence.*
   a) theology.
   b) cosmology.
   c) moral teaching.
   d) definition of time and space, special language.

2. *Communion.*
   Means and occasions for communion with God, frequent contact with fellow Catholics, and solidarity with both those who have gone before us and Catholics throughout the world.

3. *Sacralizing the identity of each person.*
   Identifying the individual as a temple of the Holy Spirit, a bearer of the name of a patron saint, and as a member of both the parish and the larger Church.

4. *Relating to critical experiences of life and services for life.*
   Birth, marriage, suffering, death, education, health care, financial relief, counselling, family life—through rites and the direct providing of services.

5. *Promoting public witness.*
   Signs of religious profession and Church membership.

6. *Fostering a sense of mission.*
   Militancy in the face of enemies and counter-forces.

7. *Encouraging sacrifice.*
   Promoting sacrifice for personal development (fasting, abstinence, various penitential acts) and for the good of the Church community (parish support, mission support, support for the works of charity).

These are some of the central elements of the Church community of the past without the specific form they took in past decades. In our current effort to develop Church community, we do well to reflect on these elements and to consider whether all or some of them must be redeveloped today, if in a different form. As an aid to this reflection, let us look at some of the changes that have occurred in our society which have contributed to the passing of traditional community life and which will condition any attempts to restore community.

Conditions Affecting Community Development

We obviously cannot detail all of the social and cultural conditions that affect religion and Church membership today. But we can specify some of the structural changes that have occurred, even with little comment or elaboration. They include: 1. Access of Catholics to many other providers of meaning and services. 2. Greater dependence of Church services on public funding (health, educational, social service funds and reimbursement). 3. Considerable mobility, residentially and economically. 4. Expansion of non-Church movements regarding social identity and morality (peace movement, civil rights movement, women's movement, ethnic movement, etc.). 5. Fewer services contained within the parish area—children are not born at home, the dying are not cared for at home, schools, health services, welfare services, and shopping are more concentrated in regional centers. 6. New critical conditions in people's lives—parenting in smaller families, changing roles of women, occupation as a source of creative identity, larger numbers of longer-living elderly not living with other members of the family, and the like.

The result of these changes is that many of the elements that made the Church community so significant in the past simply are not contained within the parish or larger Church. Of course, there still are many parish schools and Church universities, hospitals and social service institutions. Nonetheless, the mobility of Catholics, their social mobility and residential mobility, makes them less dependent on Church services and less loyal to the communities of the past. This is not a criticism. It is simply a fact; the significance of the Church community will depend on its ability to relate to the broader society and the new institutions and circles within which people live their lives.

In addition to these structural changes in Church and society, dramatic attitudinal changes have occurred. Let me point to just three of these shifts that will affect Church community development:
1. Decline in the authority of tradition. 2. Increased demands for participation in decisions affecting one's life. 3. Growing awareness that power in society is located in larger, more inaccessible institutional structures.

Tradition, "this is the way we've always done it," simply is not a very persuasive argument, and to the extent that the moral force of a community is identified as the force of tradition, the authority of the community is diminished. This is true for the family, for the Church, or for other communities. This is not the same thing as saying that a group's tradition has nothing to offer, for the tradition may be reinterpreted and translated to meet contemporary criteria for wisdom and pertinence. But the simple restatement of the tradition meets little acceptance.

Similarly, the democratic revolution affects the Church—people expect to be heard concerning the decisions affecting their lives, not simply listened to, but really heard. There is always the danger of a least-common-denominator result of broad participation, but if participation in the life of the community is not simply a means but an end in Church life, then we must find better ways to relate this form of participation to the two-edged sword of the gospel, to the contributions of experts, and to the need to be faithful to our tradition.

So also is there a need to make the power of institutions accessible to people. The Church, like all other institutions in our society, has undergone extensive centralization in expanding, higher-level, organizational structures. While the numbers of church-going Catholics, priests, sisters, parochial schools and other units of the Church have all decreased, the numbers of offices and officials in chanceries and national offices have increased. In the Church and in other institutions, people feel that power and decision-making is increasingly remote. Ways must be found to make all power more accessible and thereby more accountable to the people.

To review, the restoration of Church community must take

into account all of the central elements of a religious community, and must include the three dimensions of being a symbolic value community. It must both be much more in touch with forces and institutions of the larger society, and able to make the enduring vision of the gospel more immediately relevant to a much more participative Church membership. Serious attempts are being made in these directions. Let us look at some of these attempts at significant Church community.

Current Attempts at Church Community

There are many efforts being made to restore the vitality of Church community. These include opportunities for a renewed experience of communion of faith, attempts to relate to developments in science and society, new ways of relating to essential services, increased participation in church and community power and decision-making, and attempts to relate to new boundaries of space and time.[6] Let us review these developments briefly.

1. Toward Greater Communion
Two movements place their stress on the achievement of a deeper sense of communion: the charismatic movement and the marriage encounter movement. The charismatic movement most directly focuses on communion with God, on the fostering of mystical experience, personal expressiveness and fellowship with others who experience similar union with God and are similarly expressive.

The marriage encounter movement focuses on greater affective expression between husbands and wives and related to this, greater expressiveness in relation to God, to children and to others.

Both are communal but not social, i.e., they foster communion but prescind from questions of social identity, social structures (of Church or society), or of social action. Neither are they analytic. They do not deal with attempts at greater conceptual clarity in defining reality.

There is much power in both movements because of the need

to experience transcendence and communion. They tend not to be parochial, though both show signs of trying to relate more to local parish life.

2. *Other Expressions of Communion*

There are other communion-oriented programs, various kinds of encounter programs, designed to foster deeper experience of God in one's life and deeper experience of fellowship. Among the most prevalent are teen-age encounter programs. Like the former, these involve a kind of conversion experience through which individuals face the demands of radical commitment to God.

3. *Reflection Communities*

A third, slowly spreading trend is toward the development within parishes of smaller groups that will engage in shared reflection on faith and the Scriptures, reflection on members' life experiences and situations, and, among some, common action in regard to events and developments in the local community. These are in the consciousness-raising category and specifically entail an effort to interpret experience in the light of faith and to find the basis for individual or collective decisions and action.

Most prominent among these are the *communidades de base*, or base communities coming to the United States from Latin America but also prevalent in sections of Africa. Actually, there is evidence of such groups in almost every section of the world among Christian and non-Christian groups. There are many other examples of such small, intra-parish communities but these are more individually developed approaches in various parishes around the country.[7]

These may be considered as current replacements for the Jocist groups (YCS, YCW, CFM), but they are not restricted to a specific status (student, worker, married couple) and tend to be somewhat more explicitly holistic, i.e., dealing with all aspects of the members' lives in relation to each other. Emphasis here is not on communion but on reflection (with a more critical analysis of society) and on action, though communion does arise from the trust required for continuous reflection/action and by the fellowship engendered.

4. *Social Action*

A further development is the involvement of parishes, especially in low income communities and changing neighborhoods, in both the delivery of services and the impact of institutional forces. This renews the relationship of the Church to essential services, either in the development of publicly funded service programs (community health programs, Neighborhood Youth Corps, poverty agencies, housing sponsorship and tenant organizing and other services) or in advocacy groups impacting institutions related to the area (banks, government services, real estate agencies and owners, hospitals, utilities, and the like). In some instances, the new service is the result of diocesan agency (especially Catholic Charities) and parish cooperation, in others it is the parish itself that is the actor. In some instances the parish collaborates with other community groups. Some such action is, in effect, the collaboration of institutional leaders, while other action involves Alinsky-style multi-issue people's organizations.

Frequently, these activities are non-religious by definition and it has been the experience of many Church people that they tend to be coalition building rather than community building, lacking either enduring fellowship or the kind of reflection and value-commitment necessary for community. Emphasis is on action and on human development and, as such, indicates that Church life is concerned with secular structures, human services and human development.

5. *Revalorizing the Sacraments as Expressions of Commitment and Community*

There is widespread development of new approaches to baptism, confirmation, penance and the Eucharist. Preparation more extensively involves parents, clarifies the demands of authentic participation in these sacraments, elicits clearer testimony of commitment, and stresses the communal character of the sacraments. Again, this seems especially true in minority communities, but the trend is present everywhere. These efforts at best embrace all the diversions of a symbolic value community, though there are tendencies both to emphasize information (doctrine) and to reduce the preparation to presence at a certain number of required sessions.[8]

6. *Broadening Participation in Decision-Making and Ministry*

Answering the need to foster greater participation in a Church that is necessarily more of a voluntary community, are structures for participation in decision-making (parish councils or other committees, area councils, diocesan councils), and opportunities for participation in ministry—deacons, lectors, ministers of the Eucharist, religious education positions, social service roles, and other forms of staff and volunteer expansion. There is a tendency for the decision-making councils to be unrelated to considerations of ultimate meaning or communion—the celebration, ritual, or affective life of the Church community.

7. *Expanding the Span of Ministry*

In some areas of the country and especially in regard to social action, there is a movement toward inter-parish regional efforts, efforts to relate better to both the level of a problem and the existence of regional communities. In some few instances, this involves specifically regional staff that operates at the level of the larger area.

8. *Expanding the Scope of Ministry*

Parish ministry is broadening not only its span through inter-parish collaboration but also its scope by relating to new issues. These include the needs of increasing numbers of elderly, the crisis of separation and divorce, and some of the social action issues, such as disinvestment of neighborhoods by financial institutions, voter registration, housing development and other issues.

9. *Parish Teams*

A further example of the search for community is among the ministerial personnel. More frequently, the staff of a parish see themselves as a communal group, sharing responsibility and ministry. There is also a tendency to share prayer, fellowship, and recreation. This is reflective of both the decline of hierarchical structures and the need to experience greater support in the exercise of ministry. There is a tendency for these teams to place great emphasis on the achievement of community among themselves as distinct from the sharing of skills for more effective ministry (e.g., members tend to choose each other in this way).[9] Some of the best community building in parishes has occurred where there is little attention paid to community development among the ministers.

To which of the elements of community life do these developments contribute? The charismatic movement, the marriage encounter movement, and more communal approaches to preparation for, and reception of, the sacraments all contribute to the need to experience communion. In their attempts to elicit deeper expressions of faith, and in their gathering people around these expressions of faith, they foster communion with God and communion with other believers. A similar contribution is made by other forms of spiritual-encounter groups. These groups also tend to foster greater participation in decision-making because they are less hierarchical in structure.

There are further and broader efforts to increase participation in decision-making through various councils, community organizing and parish teams, and in ministry itself through the opening up of various types of parish ministry to religious and lay people.

Social action efforts are leading the Church into new relations with essential services, new ways of providing these services, an advocacy role in relationship to the delivery of services, or as organizer of popular power to deal with the institutional power that controls services.

The expanding span of ministry to regional, inter-parish levels is enabling the Church to relate to the way in which social space is actually divided and to the ways social life, government, and services are organized.

The development of reflection communities provides an opportunity for the parish to relate to the critical questions of people's lives, including family and work, to draw on the resources of faith as interpretive and orienting for experience, and to provide a context for communion that includes a social search for meaning and a critique of action.

A parish that attempted to include within its life all of these elements would have made great strides toward the recovery of community. It would, thereby, have acquired a surer basis for grounding people's religious identity, for the Catholic in such a parish would find himself/herself related to a broad range of reflection, expression and action, pertinent to the basic issues of life and the significant forces of society. Obviously, these developments are not all integrated with each other and it is unlikely that the same parishioners would be found in all the types of activity. Nonetheless, the very presence of these diverse movements would suggest the many dimensions of authentic Christian life and Church community. In fact, we might argue that any serious attempt at Church community will include some form of charismatic life, communal celebration of the sacraments, development of internal forms of reflection, and participation in decision-making, social action and cooperation in regional, inter-parish action.

Still there are some characteristics of Church community which require further attention. And this brings us to our final section.

Further Directions for Church Community

Where do we need to go from here? What are the elements and dimensions of parish and Church community that still need attention? Of course, it would make a great difference if some of the developments already mentioned were more widespread. Unfortunately, this is not the case. Still, in addition to the developments we have reviewed, are there other developments that might contribute to a new form of Church community? Let us look at just a few.

One development would be simply—and not so simply—taking into account all the elements and dimensions that constitute the Church as a significant symbolic value community. This would mean a systematic attempt to reflect on what constitutes such a community, where a particular parish's strengths and weaknesses are, and where new efforts are necessary. Of course, efforts to meet all the demands of community exceed the limitations of the staff of most parishes. It will only be by increasing participation in parish life and ministry that these demands can be met.

A second area that needs considerable attention is our ability to deal with and provide ultimate meaning. In part this is a question of clarifying the basic values to which we are called by the Gospel, and by the elucidation of the Gospel through tradition. But it also involves our ability to speak about ultimate realities in the light of faith, and our ability to speak about the ultimate significance of the ordinary. What, for example, do we have to say about death? Surely, the help provided by new approaches to death and dying and continuous efforts to deal with the ethical questions about death are valuable and important. But are we able to speak clearly about the meaning of death and are we able to express, not only Christian hope concerning death, but also the tragedy of death? Similarly, while we attempt to fight poverty and suffering and to counsel in times of distress and failure, do we have anything to say, in word or rite, that can provide meaning for what seems so devoid of meaning?

If this is a problem regarding ultimate realities, what about the meaning we offer concerning the pressing ordinary realities of life: sex, work, material possessions, family? Are there new ways in which the expressions of faith and of a community of faith must speak about these critical elements of life?

In our ministry, we must relate to secular sciences and structures, the understanding and resources available from psychology, sociology, medicine and social services, but we must also deal with the questions of meaning that transcend these forces. And it will be necessary, if we are to develop significant Church community, to develop much more in this area of ultimate meaning.

A third area for further development is in possibilities of communion that are not so dependent on the high levels of commitment and involvement required by most current attempts at communion. These will be structures for contact and participation by a broader constituency. This is as true of the parish team as it is of the parish community. Besides parish teams based on the common search for some affective community, we need teams that are based on commitment to shared work and that are assembled with a clear eye to the diverse skills needed for ministry in a particular parish. Similarly, we need many more ways for people to be able to do things for one another and to be in contact with each other. Besides the more intense experience of communion achieved by the charismatic and encounter groups, there could be significant experience of communion in shared work and celebrations that allow more room to people for varying degrees of expressiveness, of faith, of openness and even of commitment.

A fourth area for redevelopment is that of sacrifice for the good of the community. American Catholics have been extraordinary in their willingness to sacrifice so that they might contribute to the good of others and the work of the Church. This has been evident in support for social services, for education, for missions and in many other ways. The Campaign for Human Development is one important recent example of this. But, as government has assumed larger responsibility for services, as schools have tended to become distinct budgetary units in parishes, and as ethnic differences divide the middle-class Catholic from the poor, there is increased need to restore the same sense of sacrifice for the good of the whole body of Christ. This may require more occasions for celebrating our oneness with each other across ethnic and economic lines, and clearer evidence of the special role the Church plays relative to essential services. But a community that does not call for sacrifice will be a weak community.

There are many other areas where we need new developments to restore the Church community. But these may be suggestive of the directions necessary for Church community development. What is included here is already a very demanding agenda. Considerable effort by an expanding corps of parish ministers is required if we will incarnate the community of faith and of life in the Spirit of Christ in the flesh of today's world. The demands are great and the scope of parish community life outlined here strains our imagination and resources. But we would be remiss if we did not acknowledge the full scope of the task.

NOTES

1. Gail Sheehy, *Passages* (New York: E. P. Dutton, 1976).
2. For an analysis of symbols, see Rollo May, "The Significance of Symbols," in Rollo May ed., *Symbolism in Religion and Literature* (New York: George Braziller, 1960), pp. 11-49.
3. Clyde Kluckhohn, "Values and Value-Orientations in the Theory of Action," in Parsons and Shils, eds., *Toward A General Theory of Action* (New York, 1962), p. 395.

4. A more familiar expression in sociology is a "total" community, a term coined by Erving Goffmann to describe a community that is completely enclosed. The term "comprehensive" seems more adequate to the Church of the past, since it was not completely enclosed at any time.

5. An interesting analysis of utopian communities, with many analogies to our discussion and especially to previous forms of religious orders is Rosabeth Moss Kanter's *Commitment and Community* (Cambridge: Harvard U. Press, 1972). Of similar value is Peter Berger's discussion of "plausibility structures," those systems that include a network of beliefs and relationships that provide a meaning-context for life; see Peter Berger, *Rumor of Angels* (Garden City, N.Y.: Doubleday Anchor, 1970), pp. 36ff.

6. It is in just such a direction that we are led by Vatican II and especially by the documents, *Lumen Gentium* and *Gaudium et Spes*.

7. See, among other sources, the following regarding small or base communities: Jose Ignacio Torres, ed., *Communidades Cristianas de Base*, 2nd ed., (Bogota: Indo-American Press Service, 1971); James F. Bolger, "Communidades Cristianas de Base in Theory and Practice: A Realistic Pastoral Option," *The Dunwoodie Review*, vol. 14:1, 1974, pp. 23-42; Joseph K. Donohue "Communidad de Base: A Resource for Social Action," *Clergy Report* (newsletter of the Office of Pastoral Research, Archdiocese of New York), February 1977, pp. 7-8; Edgar Beltran, "Ecclesial Communidades de Base," *Clergy Report,* May 1976, pp. 1 ff. See related proposals and projects: Albert Ottenweller, "A Call to Restructure the Parish," *Clergy Report,* April 1976, pp. 10-11; Ralph Kiefer, "A Church of Diversity and Caring," *National Catholic Reporter,* October 4, 1974.

8. One study of present and proposed baptismal policy is *Baptismal Preparation in the Archdiocese* done by the Office of Pastoral Research of the Archdiocese of New York, 1976.

9. See a discussion of this in this writer's ''Community and Team,'' *Clergy Report*, February 1974.